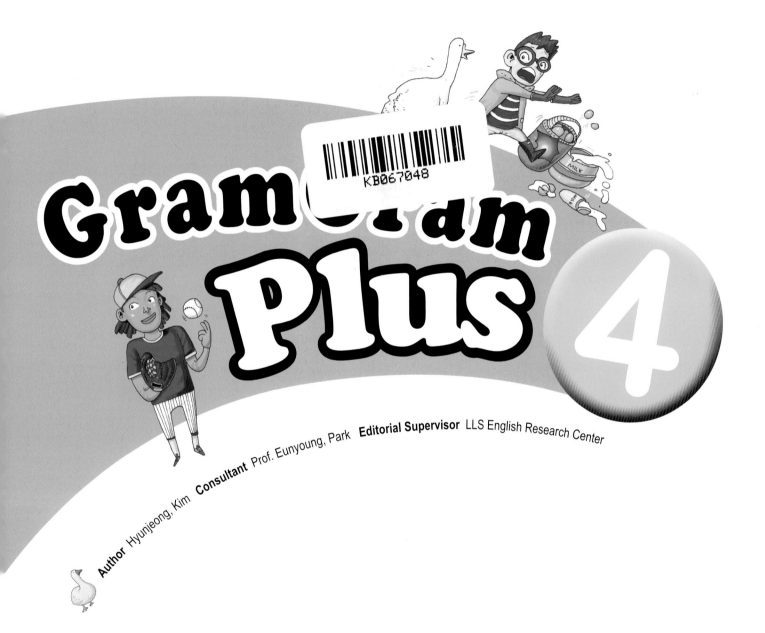

Gram Gram Plus 4

Author Hyunjeong, Kim **Consultant** Prof. Eunyoung, Park **Editorial Supervisor** LLS English Research Center

J PLUS
Language Publishing Co.

Have Fun and Enjoy
the
GRAM GRAM PLUS Series

Welcome to the GRAM GRAM PLUS Series.

This is an introductory grammar series designed to be fun and easy for young learners. It is also designed to promote accurate English speaking and writing skills.

Korean students have traditionally learned English grammar through rote memorization. However, I believe that grammar learning is more effectively realized when instruction is paired with practice. With clear explanations, imaginative illustrations, enjoyable grammar activities and games, the GRAM GRAM PLUS Series allows students to enjoy English grammar as they learn how to use it properly.

The GRAM GRAM PLUS Series provides students with ample opportunities to both practice and improve their English.

Author: Hyunjeong, Kim

Supervisor's Recommendation

Traditionally, many language teachers have taught English grammar according to the Grammar Translation Method. In grammar-translation classes, students learn grammatical rules and then apply those rules by translating sentences between the target language and their native language. Advanced students may be required to translate whole texts word-for-word. However, at the height of the Communicative Approach to language learning in the 1980s and early 1990s, it became fashionable in some quarters to deride so-called "old-fashioned" methods and, in particular, something broadly labeled "Grammar Translation". Nevertheless, we can't ignore grammar in language teaching and learning. In that sense, this series can help both teachers and students by presenting grammar in a communicative way, which can be a very fascinating way to learn English grammar. With a lot of pictures, cartoons, games, and activities, children will be able to 'acquire' English grammar, not to 'study' grammar. I hope that many kids will enjoy this joyful process!

Consultant: Prof. Eunyoung, Park

(Ph. D. in English Education / Professor at Methodist Theological University)

GRAM GRAM
PLUS BOOK 4

Unit	Title		Grammar	Topic/Theme	Vocabulary	문법포인트
1	I Want Some Cheese	Quantifiers & Adverbs	- Quantifiers 1: some / any	Grocery	- vegetables, fruits, seafood, dairy products, baverages, meat	
2	He Drinks A Lot Of Water		- Quantifiers 2: many / much / a lot of	Food	- nuts, junk food, sweets, rice & soup, coffee & tea, steak & salad	
3	He Speaks English Well		- Adverbs: early / well / quietly / late, etc.	School Life	- speak English, explain, raise a hand, sit down, solve a problem, take notes	
4	I Always Walk To School		- Adverbs of Frequency: always / often / never / usually / sometimes	Daily Rountine	- get up, take a shower, have breakfast, pack a schoolbag, do homework, go to bed	
5	I'm Milking A Cow!	Basic Sentence Forms	- Sentence Structures 1: "Subject + Verb + Object" love, like, make, pla, etc.	Things To Do On The Farm	- feed a calf, shear sheep, milk a cow, unload a truck, pick apples, gather eggs	
6	My Friends Sent Me Presents		- Sentence Structures 2: "Subject + Verb + I.O. + D.O." give, send, buy, etc.	School Bazaar	- give, lend, bring, sell, show, pass, teach, buy, send - a CD, sneakers, a T-shirt, photos, a model robot, comic books	
7	Look At That Guy Playing The Guitar		- Sentence Structures 3: "Subject + Verb + O + O.C."	Outdoor Rock Festival	- see, look at, hear, listen to, watch, feel, sense - play Frisbee, wait in line, have one's hair cut, go to a rock festival, unfold a blanket, perform	
8	Please Make Greta Set The Table		- Sentence Structures 4: "Subject + Verb + O + O.C."	Birthday Party	- have, let, make, get, help, keep, etc. - clean up the trash, decorate the room, serve the food, blow out the candles, have one's hair cut	

4 GRAM GRAM PLUS BOOK 4

Unit	Title		Grammar	Topic/Theme	Vocabulary	문법포인트
9	I Enjoy Watching Cartoons	Basic Sentence Forms	- Verb Pattern 1: "Verb + Base Verb+ ing" enjoy, stop, finish, like, love, begin, hate, go, keep, etc.	Hobbies	- make a model airplane, watch cartoons, take a picture, chat with, make cupcakes, play the guitar	
10	I Want To Do My Hair		- Verb Pattern 2: "Verb + To Base Verb" want, decide, plan, hope, need, promise, would like, forget, learn, ask, prepare, remember, etc.	Summer Vacation Plan	- get a haircut, go on a trip, go surf, see the paintings, learn French, watch the fireworks	
11	Who Will Do The Presentation?		- Question Words: who, which, whose, where, what, when, why, how	School Cooking Contest	- attend the contest, do a presentation, work in groups, win a contest, try food	
12	If You Don't Hurry Up…		- First Conditionals: "If"	Daily Rountine & House Chores	- get bad marks, tidy a room, have bad sight, get pocket money, mow the lawn, feel ill	
13	I Am As Tall As Steve	Comparatives & Superlatives	- Comparatives: "As ~ As / Not As ~ As"	Adjectives Of Personality	- strong, shy, smart, talkative, friendly, popular	
14	Which One Is Faster?		- Comparatives: "-er / More ~ Than"	Opposites 1	- fast - slow, expensive - cheap, fat - thin, young - old, hungry - full, high - short	
15	What Is The Tallest Tower?		- Superlatives: "The -est / The Most ~"	Opposites 2	- hot - cold, old - new, wide - narrow, tall - short, heavy - light, famous	
16	Have You Ever Cooked A Turkey?	The Simple Present Perfect	- The Simple Present Perfect: Experience "have(has) (never) + p.p." "Have + S + ever + p.p. ~?"	Thanksgiving Party	- Past Particles: been, come, played, etc. - pop Indian corn, bake a pumpkin pie, cook a turkey, peel potatoes, keep one's diary, eat with chopsticks	

Hello! I'm Gram!

STEP 1

GRAM'S TALK

해당 유닛의 핵심 주제와 관련된 단어와 어구를 하나의 재미있는 상황으로 설정하여 삽화로 제시하였습니다. 한눈에 보이는 그림을 통해 핵심 단어들을 쉽고 빠르게 파악할 수 있습니다.

GRAM'S Expressions

해당 유닛의 주제와 연관된 핵심 단어, 어구를 제시하였습니다. 단어를 듣고 알맞은 그림을 찾는활동을 하며, 주제 중심 핵심 단어들을 체크해 봅니다.

Easy to Follow

6 STEP
Lesson Process

STEP 2

GRAM POINT

해당 유닛의 문법 포인트를 간단한 설명과 도표로 제시하였습니다. 문법 체계에 대한 분석 없이 하나의 문법 사항을 하나의 도표로 빠르게 학습할 수 있습니다. 친절한 GRAM의 한국말 설명은 문법 포인트에 대한 빠른 이해를 도와줍니다.

GRAM CHECK-UP

위에서 확인한 문법 포인트를 간단한 확인문제를 통해 확인해 볼 수 있습니다.

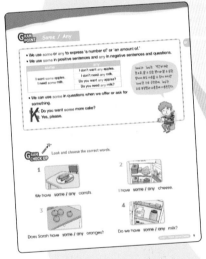

STEP 3

GRAM PRACTICE

해당 유닛의 주제 중심 단어와 문법 포인트를 확인할 수 있는 다양한 형식의 액티비티를 제시하였습니다. 빈칸 채우기, 알맞은 말 고르기, 표 보고 문장 완성하기, 잘못된 표현 고치기 등의 다양한 형식의 액티비티를 통해 앞서 익힌 단어와 문법 포인트를 쉽고 재미있게 정리해 볼 수 있습니다.

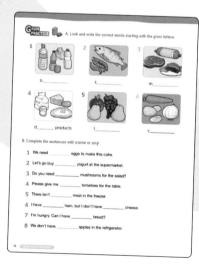

STEP 6

FUNNY GRAM

해당 유닛의 문법 포인트와 핵심 단어를 활용한 게임을 제시하였습니다.
다양한 유형의 게임을 통해 해당 유닛의 문법 포인트와 핵심 단어를 마지막으로 정리, 확인할 수 있도록 하였습니다.

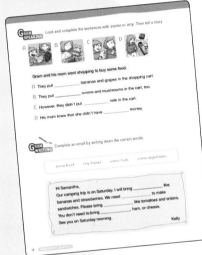

STEP 5

GRAM SPEAKING

그림보고 질문에 답하기/연계질문에 답하기/그림묘사하기/문제 해결하기 등 'Speaking Activity'를 제시하였습니다.

GRAM WRITING

그림 선택해서 묘사하기/그림 세부 묘사하기/편지쓰기/추론하여 글쓰기 등의 'Writing Activity'를 제시하였습니다. 앞서 익힌 '문법'을 실제로 '활용'할 수 있는 기회를 통해 실용적인 문법 학습은 물론, 각종 시험에 대한 대비도 할 수 있습니다

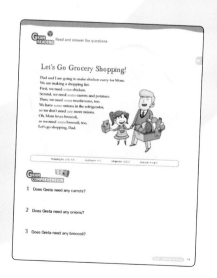

STEP 4

GRAM READING

해당 유닛의 문법 포인트가 포함된 80자 이내의 리딩 지문을 제시하였습니다. 익숙하고도 재미있는 상황으로 구성된 리딩 지문을 읽으며 문법이 실제 활용되는 예를 자연스럽게 확인할 수 있습니다.

GRAM Comprehension

읽은 내용을 확인해 볼 수 있는 주관식 문제를 제시하였습니다. 해당 유닛의 문법 포인트를 활용할 수 있도록 하였습니다.

일러두기

Unit 01

I Want Some Cheese

Mom, do we have any bread?

No, we don't.

Then, do we have any cheese?

No.

Do we have any eggs?

Sorry. We don't have any eggs.

Then what do we have?

We have many things to buy!

GRAM Expressions ABC Listen and number the pictures in order. Track 3

vegetables

fruits

seafood

dairy products

beverages

meat

GRAM POINT — Some / Any

- We use some or any to express 'a number of' or 'an amount of.'
- We use some in positive sentences and any in negative sentences and questions.

some	any
I want some apples. I need some milk.	I don't want any apples. I don't need any milk. Do you want any apples? Do you need any milk?

'some'과 'any'는 '약간의'라는 뜻으로, 셀 수 있는 명사와 셀 수 없는 명사에 모두 사용할 수 있어. 하지만 'some'은 주로 긍정문에, 'any'는 주로 부정문과 의문문에 사용된단다.

- We can use some in questions when we offer or ask for something.

Ex A: Do you want **some** more cake?
   B: Yes, please.

GRAM CHECK UP

Look and choose the correct words.

1

We have some / any carrots.

2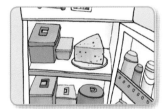

I have some / any cheese.

3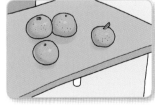

Does Sarah have some / any oranges?

4

Do we have some / any milk?

A. Look and write the correct words starting with the given letters.

1

b_____

2

s_____

3

m_____

4

d_____ products

5

f_____

6

v_____

B. Complete the sentences with *some* or *any*.

1 We need _____ eggs to make this cake.

2 Let's go buy _____ yogurt at the supermarket.

3 Do you need _____ mushrooms for the salad?

4 Please give me _____ tomatoes for the table.

5 There isn't _____ meat in the freezer.

6 I have _____ ham, but I don't have _____ cheese.

7 I'm hungry. Can I have _____ bread?

8 We don't have _____ apples in the refrigerator.

01

Let's Go Grocery Shopping!

Dad and I are going to make chicken curry for Mom.
We are making a shopping list.
First, we need some chicken.
Second, we need some carrots and potatoes.
Then, we need some mushrooms, too.
We have some onions in the refrigerator,
so we don't need any more onions.
Oh, Mom loves broccoli,
so we need some broccoli, too.
Let's go shopping, Dad.

| shopping list 쇼핑 목록 | mushroom 버섯 | refrigerator 냉장고 | broccoli 브로콜리 |

GRAM COMPREHENSION

1 Does Greta need any carrots?

_____

2 Does Greta need any onions?

_____

3 Does Greta need any broccoli?

_____

GRAM SPEAKING Look and complete the sentences with *some* or *any*. Then tell a story.

A  B  C  D

Gram and his mom went shopping to buy some food.

A They put _____ bananas and grapes in the shopping cart.

B They put _____ onions and mushrooms in the cart, too.

C However, they didn't put _____ milk in the cart.

D His mom knew that she didn't have _____ money.

 **GRAM WRITING** Complete an email by writing down the correct words.

some food	any bread	some fruits	some vegetables

Hi Samantha,

Our camping trip is on Saturday. I will bring _____ like

bananas and strawberries. We need _____ to make

sandwiches. Please bring _____ like tomatoes and onions.

You don't need to bring _____, ham, or cheese.

See you on Saturday morning.

Kelly

Grocery Shopping

Cut out the shopping bag and paste it below.
Cut out the picture cards. Choose 5 cards and put them in the bag. Then, ask and answer the questions using *some* and *any*.

Do you have any potatoes?

Yes, I do.
(No, I don't.)

I have some carrots.

I don't have any apples.

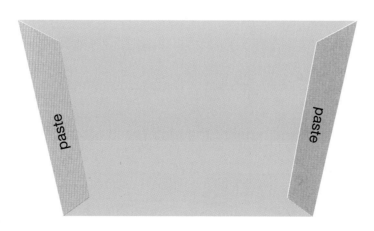

paste

paste

He Drinks A Lot Of Water

Unit 02

GRAM TALK Track 5 ☐ Listen ☐ Repeat ☐ Role play

GRAM Expressions Track 6 ABC Listen and number the pictures in order. Track 7

nuts   junk food   sweets   rice & soup   coffee & tea   steak & salad

GRAM POINT — Many / Much / A lot of

- We use many, much, or a lot of to express 'a large number of' or 'a large amount of.'

Countable (plural) Noun		Uncountable Nouns	
many bananas	many carrots	much food	much soup
a lot of bananas	a lot of carrots	a lot of food	a lot of soup

02

- We usually use much in negative sentences and questions.
  Ex I don't need much cheese. / Do you drink much tea?

- We use How many ~? or How much ~? to ask questions about number or amount.
  Ex How many eggs do you have?
  How much water do you have?

'many, much, a lot of' 는 모두 '많은' 이라는 뜻이야. 'many' 는 셀 수 있는 명사 앞에, 'much' 는 셀 수 없는 명사 앞에, 그리고 'a lot of' 는 셀 수 있는 명사와 셀 수 없는 명사에 모두 사용할 수 있어.

GRAM CHECK UP
 Look and choose the correct words.

1

Annie has many / much sweets.

2

We had a lot of / many steak.

3

How much / many milk do you drink a day?

4

How many / much oranges do you eat every day?

A. Look and match the pictures with the correct words.

1

2

3

4

5

6

• nuts

• sweets

• steak & salad

• rice & soup

• coffee & tea

• junk food

B. Complete the sentences with *many* or *much*.

1 I usually add _____ nuts to my salad.

2 We need _____ different breads for the party.

3 Wendy doesn't have _____ vegetables.

4 How _____ cookies did you eat?

5 Annie drinks _____ coffee every day.

6 How _____ orange juice do we have?

7 Irene made _____ delicious food for us.

8 I wasn't hungry. I didn't eat _____ rice.

 **Read and answer the questions.**

Let's Eat A Balanced Diet!

We should eat a balanced diet for our health.
We should eat a lot of fresh fruits and
vegetables every day.
They have a lot of vitamins and minerals.
However, we should not eat too much
junk food like hamburgers, pizza, and
fried chicken.
Junk food has too many calories
and too much fat.
Junk food has a lot of salt, too.
Eat a balanced diet and keep healthy.

---

balanced 균형 잡힌   diet 식단   health 건강   mineral 미네랄   calorie 칼로리   fat 지방   healthy 건강한

1 Should we eat many fresh fruits?   a lot of

_____

2 Should we eat much junk food?

_____

3 Does junk food have many calories?

_____

GRAM SPEAKING

Look and answer the questions using the given hints.

1

Does Gram have any cookies?

Yes. _____

a lot of

2

Did Greta drink a lot of water?

No. _____

much

3

How many oranges does Gram have?

_____

five

GRAM WRITING

Look and write the correct expressions.

1 Gram was in a pizza restaurant with his friends.

There was _____ pizza.

a lot of / very much

2 When Gram got home, he said that he was hungry.

His mom asked, "_____ pizza did you eat?

How many / How much

3 Gram answered, "I didn't eat _____ because I wasn't hungry.

many pizza / much pizza

I drank _____ ."

many cokes / a lot of coke

Word Ladder

Fill the ladder with the words below. Then, ask and answer the questions. If you have the food, cross out the name on your ladder. The player who crosses out five words first is the winner.

Do you have many bananas?

Yes, I do. / No, I don't.

FINISH

many _____
many _____
much _____
much _____
many _____
many _____
much _____
many _____

START

He Speaks English Well

  ☐ Listen   ☐ Repeat   ☐ Role play

   Listen and number the pictures in order.

speak English   explain   raise a hand   sit down   solve a problem   take notes

G RAM POINT — Early / Well / Quietly

- We use adverbs early, well, quietly, etc. to express how we do something or how something happens.

  Ex I go to bed early.   The bus arrived late.

- We usually add –ly to an adjective to form the adverb.

–ly	slow – slow**ly** quiet – quiet**ly** careful – careful**ly**	quick – quick**ly** loud – loud**ly**
(-y) ➜ i + -ly	easy – eas**ily**	happy - happ**ily**
Irregular	early – **early** fast – **fast**	late – **late** good – **well** hard – **hard**

부사는 주로 동사나 부사를 꾸며주는 말이야. 형용사 뒤에 '-ly' 를 붙여 부사를 만들기도 하지만, 'early, late, hard, fast' 같은 단어들은 형용사와 부사의 형태가 같다는 점을 꼭 기억하자!

Ex Nicole is **quiet**. Nicole speaks quietly.
Tim is a **good** soccer player. Tim plays soccer well.

 **Look and choose the correct words.**

1

Gram always talks   loudly / quietly .

2

Greta solves math problems   fast / slowly .

3

Greta walks   fast / slowly   in the classroom.

4

Greta sings   badly / well .

 **A. Look and complete the sentences with the correct verbs.**

| explain | raise | speak | take | sit | solve |

1 Please _____ down

2 Please _____ your hand.

3 Please _____ notes.

4 Please _____ this problem.

5 Please _____ to us.

6 Please _____ in English.

B. Correct the mistakes in red and rewrite the sentences.

1 Kelly plays the piano good.

➡ _____.

2 We should take notes careful.

➡ _____.

3 Nick always tries to study hardly.

➡ _____.

4 Mr. Hans explains English grammar easy.

➡ _____.

5 Please sit down quick and read the questions.

➡ _____.

Rules For The Test!

Take your seat quickly and listen carefully.
Pass out the tests quickly.
When you have a question, please raise
your hand quietly.
Don't talk loudly with your classmates.
Read and answer the questions carefully.
After the test, leave the classroom quietly.

take a seat 자리에 앉다   pass out 전달하다, 건네주다   classmate 반 친구   leave 떠나다

 **COMPREHENSION**   Using the rules above, correct the following sentences.

1 The students should take their seats slowly.

_____

2 The students should talk loudly when they have a question.

_____

3 The students should leave the classroom fast after the test.

_____

 **Look and answer the questions using the given words.**

> Q: Is Greta a good singer?
> A: <u>Yes, she is. She sings well.</u>
>   well

1 Q: Does Greta study?

   A: Yes, _____   hard

2 Q: Does Greta talk quietly?

   A: No, _____   loudly

 **Look and complete the sentences using the given words.**

Word Box	
doing	loudly
singing	carefully
talking	quickly
listening	quietly

There are some people in the classroom.

1 The boy is _____ to the teacher _____.

2 The girl is _____ her homework _____.

3 The two boys are _____ _____.

4 The girls are _____ _____ to each other.

Sentence Search

Fill in the purple squares with the correct adverbs.

Find and circle the sentences. Then, fill in the blanks below to complete the sentences.

TAKE	SEAT	THE	GO	DOWN	NOTE	I	THE
HE	SING	SIT	STUDY	READ	WRITE	SIT	RUN
TAKE	YOUR	SEAT	QUICKLY	AND	I	DOWN	WITH
SIT	DOWN		NOTE	I	SPEAK		THE
SLEEP	ANSWER	WRITE	TEST	READ	ENGLISH	WALK	PIANO
SCHOOL	THE	PLAY	THE	SPANISH		GIVE	THEY
AND	QUESTIONS	QUESTIONS	TAKE		TAKE	ARE	STUDY
LISTEN		SOCCER	NOTE	PLAY	SINGING	THE	
GO	RUN	DON'T	TALK		READ	TEST	WITH
READ	I	WALK		IN	THE	CLASS ROOM	SEND

1 Take _____ _____ quickly.

2 _____ carefully.

3 Answer _____ _____ carefully.

4 I _____ _____ well.

5 Read _____ _____ carefully.

6 I _____ _____ quietly.

7 I _____ _____ well.

8 Don't _____ loudly.

9 They _____ _____ loudly.

10 I _____ slowly in the classroom.

I Always Walk To School

GRAM TALK

Track 13 □ Listen □ Repeat □ Role play

I always get up at 7.

Really? I never get up at 7.

It's too early for me.

I usually do my homework after school.

How about you, Gram?

I usually do my homework in the morning.

I sometimes read books before bedtime.

Oh, you too? I always read books before bedtime like you.

GRAM Expressions

Track 14 Listen and number the pictures in order. Track 15

get up

take a shower

have breakfast

pack a schoolbag

do homework

go to bed

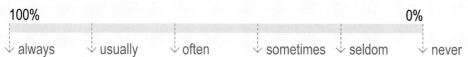

GRAM POINT — Always / Usually / Often / Never

- We use always, usually, often, sometimes, seldom, and never to express frequency.

100%   0%

↓ always   ↓ usually   ↓ often   ↓ sometimes   ↓ seldom   ↓ never

- The adverbs of frequency come **before** the (general) **verb**.

I / You / We / They	usually		get up	late.
He / She / It	usually		gets up	late.
I / You / We / They	don't	usually	get up	late.
He / She / It	doesn't	usually	get up	late.

'얼마나 자주 ~하는지'를 나타내는 말을 빈도부사라고 해! 문장에서 어느 위치에 오는지 잘 봐두자!

- However, they come **after** the verb *be* (am/is/are/was/were).

  Ex I am usually late. (O)   I usually am late. (X)

GRAM CHECK UP

Look and choose the correct words.

1

I always / never watch TV at night.

2

Ben is always / never late for school.

3

They often / never play soccer.

4

We usually / never go swimming.

RAM PRACTICE A. Look and write the correct phrases starting with the given letters.

1

_____ a schoolbag

2

do _____

3

go to _____

4

_____ a shower

5

_____ up

6

have _____

B. Rewrite the sentences with the given adverbs.

1 I have cereal for breakfast.   often

→ _____.

2 Warren takes a shower after dinner.   always

→ _____.

3 Alice and Jane are late for school.   never

→ _____.

4 Paul goes to school by bus.   sometimes

→ _____.

5 I pack my schoolbag before bed.   usually

→ _____.

 **Read and answer the questions.**

I Am An Early Bird

I always get up early.
I usually take a shower
in the morning.
After breakfast, I always
walk to school.
I am never late for school.
After school, I always do
my homework first.
Then I often play with my friends
or read books.
I always have dinner with my family.
After dinner, I seldom watch TV.
I always go to bed before 10 o'clock.

> early bird 일찍 자고 일찍 일어나는 사람   before ~이전에

 **RAM COMPREHENSION**

1 Does Gramson usually take a shower in the morning?

_____

2 Is Gramson always late for school?

_____

3 Does Gramson always go to bed after 10 o'clock?

_____

 **Look and complete the sentences with the correct words. Then tell a story.**

sometimes eat cereal	always wake up
often take the bus	always helps me

A I _____ at 7 in the morning.

B I wash my face. Then, I _____ for breakfast.

C I _____ to school, but today I walked to school.

In the evening, I usually eat dinner at 6 p.m.

D Then I do my homework. My dad _____ with my homework.

 **Complete each sentence using the given hints.**

 1

seldom / breakfast / in the morning

Gram _____.

 2

school / late for / sometimes

Greta _____.

 3

always / homework / at night

Gramson _____.

FUNNY GRAM

My Daily Schedules

Prepare a die and some game markers. During your turn, roll the die and make a sentence using the given phrase and frequency adverb.

For example, I always get up at 7 am.

Daily Time-table

START

Go!!

get up
often

have breakfast
usually

late for school
never

LOSE A TURN

play computer games
sometimes

do homework
usually

BOMB

ONE SQUARE AHEAD

have dinner
usually

read books
never

get up
usually

LOSE A TURN

pack a schoolbag
usually

go swimming
sometimes

ONE SQUARE AHEAD

walk to school
always

watch TV
seldom

wear jeans
always

LOSE A TURN

play with friends
often

go to bed
always

go shopping
often

FINISH

I Am Milking A Cow!

Unit 05

 □ Listen □ Repeat □ Role play

 Listen and number the pictures in order.

feed a calf   shear sheep   milk a cow   unload a truck   pick apples   gather eggs

• Some verbs **have** an **object**. This object is the noun receiving the action.

I	love	my dog Max.	
Sally	makes	hotdogs	well.
They	played	music	in the park.

• Here are some of the verbs which take an **object** after them.

love, like, make, play, write, eat, catch, cook, feed, find
finish, take, know, call, look for, pick, explain, describe, etc.

동사들 중에는 목적어를 한 개 가지는 동사들이 있단다. 동사 바로 뒤에 목적어가 오는 것도 꼭 기억해두자.

Ex I'm **writing a letter** to my cousin.
My sister **called me** from LA yesterday.

05

G RAM CHECK UP   Unscramble the sentences.

1

some / made / cookies

Gram _____.

2

was / the eggs / dropping

Greta _____.

3

washing / in the kitchen / the dishes / was

Gramson _____.

   **A. Fill out the blanks.**

sheep	unload	gather
pick	calf	milk

1

_____ apples

2

_____ eggs

3

feed a _____

4

_____ a truck

5

_____ a cow

6

shear _____

B. Rewrite the sentences by correcting errors.

1 Greta apples some picked.

→ Greta _____.

2 Gramson horses likes.

→ Gramson _____.

3 Gram is a cow milking.

→ Gram _____.

4 Greta reading was a comic book.

→ Greta _____.

Read and answer the questions.

Love you, Grandpa!

My grandfather has a huge farm.
Today Gramson and I helped him on his farm.
We were milking a cow.
Suddenly a big goose surprised Gramson.
He was so shocked he kicked the egg basket by
mistake. All the eggs broke.
Then the basket fell on the milk bottle.
Then the milk bottle rolled into the pigpen.
And all the pigs ran away.
What a mess!
But grandfather just hugged us smiling,
"It's OK, guys. I still love you very much."
"We love you too, Grandpa!"

kick 발로 차다	fall on 떨어지다, 넘어뜨리다	surprise 놀라게하다	run away 도망가버리다
hug 안아주다	roll into ~로 굴러 들어가다	pigpen 돼지우리	by mistake 실수로

1 What were the two boys doing when the goose appeared?

_____

2 What did Gramson kick when he was shocked?

_____

3 What did grandfather do to the children?

_____

GRAM SPEAKING Read and write down the answers using the given hints.

1 Q: What did Gram buy for Greta?

A: Gram _____

[for Greta / bought / a hairband]

2 Q: What did Greta ask to Gramson?

A: Greta _____

[a math problem / asked / to Gramson]

3 Q: What did Gramson watch?

A: Gramson _____

[a horror movie / watched]

4 Q: What did Greta read yeasterday?

A: Greta _____

[yesterday / a comic book / read]

GRAM WRITING Write descriptive sentences using the given hints.

1 Gramson _____.

English / is / to Greta / teaching

2 Greta _____.

for Gram / a camera / bought

3 Gramson _____.

how to milk a cow / asked

4 Gram _____.

a goose / received / from Gramson

5 Gramson _____.

made / cupcakes / some

JOBS ON THE FARM

Prepare a person die and 10 stickers for each player. During your turn, roll the die and choose a job for the person you got from the die. Make a sentence using the given hints from the die and the chart like "Gram cleans the pigpen on Monday(s)." If your sentence is correct, cover the job you chose on the chart with one of your stickers.

FAMILY JOB CHART

SUN	clean the pigpen	milk a cow	take care of baby chicks	unload a truck
MON	pick tomatoes	gather eggs	unload a truck	shear sheep
TUE	brush a horse	 feed a calf	clean the pigpen	milk a cow
WED	take care of baby chicks	shear sheep	gather eggs	brush a horse
THU	feed a calf	unload a truck	 milk a cow	pick tomatoes
FRI	brush a horse	gather eggs	take care of baby chicks	shear sheep
SAT	clean the pigpen	 milk a cow	pick tomatoes	feed a calf

Unit 06

My Friends Sent Me Presents

GRAM TALK Track 21 ☐ Listen ☐ Repeat ☐ Role play

> Wow, what are these?

> Birthday presents. My friends sent me presents. You know yesterday was my birthday.

> Hmm... strange. I thought your birthday is...

> Greta, can I show you my presents?

> A CD and a T-shirt and sneakers, and a comic book, and a...

> Knock, knock, knock. Is anyone there?

> Oh, hi, guys. I gave you the wrong parcels yesterday. They are all for the 'School Bazaar'. Can you give them back?

> Yes, here they are.

> Oh, my!

GRAM Expressions Track 22 ABC Listen and number the pictures in order. Track 23

a CD (give)   sneakers (lend)   a T-shirt (bring)   photos (sell)   a model robot (show)   comic books (pass)

GRAM POINT — Sentence Structures2: S + V + IO + DO

- Some verbs have two objects. The first object is the indirect object, and the second is the direct object. The indirect object refers to the person receiving something and the direct object refers to the thing that is given.

I	gave	John	my ticket	yesterday.
David	sent	his teacher	a card.	
She'll	buy	her mom	a skirt.	

- Here are some of the verbs which take two objects after them.

  give, send, buy, bring, show, pass, sell, teach, find, ask, lend, etc.

Ex James teaches me French.

  I lent my brother my laptop last night.

동사 중에는 간접목적어와 직접목적어 이렇게 두 개의 목적어가 필요한 것들이 있어. 잘 구분해서 기억하고, 어느 위치에 오는지도 잘 봐두어야 해.

06

GRAM CHECK UP — Rewrite the sentences by correcting the word order.

1  Gramson the girl sells his photos.

→ Gramson _____.

2  Greta gave some cookies the girl.

→ Greta _____.

3  Gram how to use the camera teaches Gramson.

→ Gram _____.

 **A. Fill in the blanks.**

1

2

3

4

5

6

comic books	sneakers	photos
show	Greta	bring

1 _____ Greta a model robot

2 lend Gramson his _____

3 sell the girl his _____

4 give _____ a CD

5 pass Gram the _____

6 _____ the boy a T-shirt

B. Unscramble the sentences.

1 Gram / gave / cookies / some

Greta _____.

2 his toy car / found / the boy

Gramson _____.

3 a math problem / Greta / asked

Gram _____.

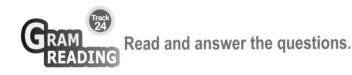
At The School Bazaar

We had a 'School Bazaar' yesterday.
Many students brought their teachers some old
and new things.
Greta brought her teacher a pink T-shirt.
I brought my teacher a brand-new backpack.
A teacher taught us how to sell our things.
And the bazaar opened.
Many students near my school came.
Gramson sold a boy his model robot first.
Gramson and I showed the students Taekwondo
performances, too.
It was a great time to learn how to share and
help each other.

| school bazaar 학교 바자회   brand-new 신품의 |
| Taegwondo performances 태권도 공연   each other 서로 |

GRAM COMPREHENSION

1   What did Greta bring?

_____

2   What did a teacher teach the students before the bazaar?

_____

3   What did Gramson sell?

_____

1

Q: Did Gramson lend Gram his T-shirt?

A: _____

2

Q: What did Gram teach Greta?

A: _____

3

Q: What did Gramson buy Greta?

A: _____

GRAM WRITING Complete the sentences using the given hints. Then write in the letter of the matching sentence.

1 Gramson _____.
   a robot magazine / Gram / bought   ◯

2 Greta _____.
   Gram / a glove / lent   ◯

3 Gram _____.
   an email / his friend / sent   ◯

4 Greta _____.
   her new sneakers /showed / Gram   ◯

5 Gramson _____.
   gave / Gram / a hotdog   ◯

A. He sent an email to his friend.

B. He gave a hotdog to Gram.

C. She showed her new sneakers to Gram.

D. He bought a robot magazine for Gram.

E. She lent a glove to Gram.

FUNNY GRAM — To The Right Person!

Cut out and prepare the indirect object die and 6 markers for each player. During your turn, roll the die and choose one of the items which belongs to the person you rolled. In 5 seconds, make a sentence which starts with "I" using the given hints like "*I gave Gram chocolate.*" If your sentence is correct, cover the item with your marker.

06

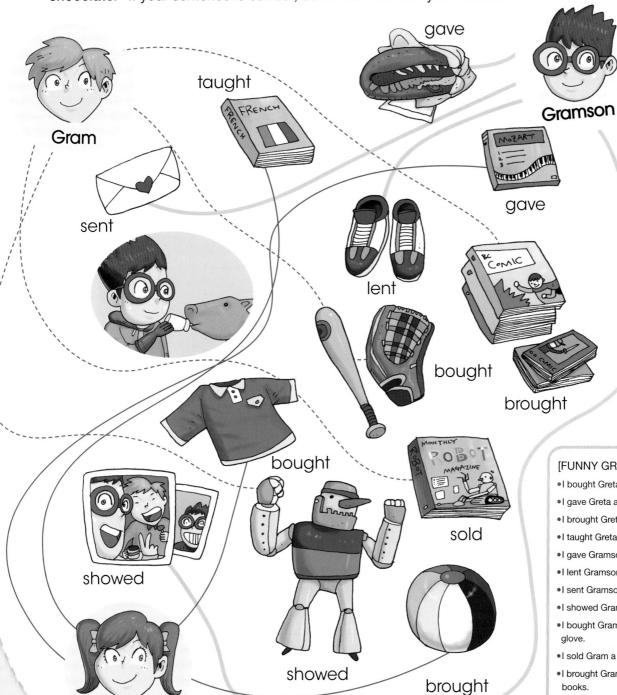

Gram

gave

taught

Gramson

sent

gave

lent

bought

brought

bought

sold

showed

showed

brought

Greta

[FUNNY GRAM EXP]
- I bought Greta a T-shirt.
- I gave Greta a CD.
- I brought Greta a ball.
- I taught Greta French.
- I gave Gramson a hotdog.
- I lent Gramson my sneakers.
- I sent Gramson a letter.
- I showed Gramson my photos.
- I bought Gram a bat and a glove.
- I sold Gram a robot magazine.
- I brought Gram a my comic books.
- I showed Gram a model robot.

Unit 07

Look At That Guy Playing The Guitar

Can you hear the rock singer singing?

Yes. Wow! Look at that guy playing the guitar. Awesome!

Did you bring the sign board, Gramson?

Ta-da! Here it is

By the way, Gram. Where is the blanket? I saw you folding the blanket this morning.

Oh, sorry. I forgot it.

It's OK. I saw a man barbecuing over there. Can we have some hotdogs?

Great! I love hotdogs!

Alright! But we have to wait in line.

Please give me your tickets.

Sure, here you are.

Oh, these are all for the flower festival.

What? Oh, Gram!

GRAM Expressions Track 26 Listen and number the pictures in order. Track 27

play Frisbee

wait in line

hold a sign

go to a rock festival

unfold a blanket

perform

Sentence Structures 3: V + O + OC

Perception Verbs

- Some verbs can be used with an object followed by a base verb + ing form or a base verb form. These verbs indicate that the subject is "focusing" on a specific object.

I	heard	you	sing.
He	saw	me	go.
They	watched	Sam	running.

- Here are some verbs of perception.

> see, look at, hear, listen to, feel, watch, sense, etc.

Ex She **looked at** James run. (Focus on her looking.)

I **listened to** the bird singing. (Focus on the bird's singing.)

[Compare: We **heard** you ~~to leave~~. (Incorrect)]

지각동사는 목적어와 목적
보어를 취하는데, 각 동사들의
쓰임에 따라 "동사 원형" 이나,
"동사 + ing" 형이 오기도 해.

Choose the correct words.

1  I saw Gram [to hold] [holding] a sign in the concert.

2  Greta watched Gramson [buy] [bought] some hotdogs.

3  Gramson listened to the girls [shouting] [to shout].

A. Write down the phrases from the box.

play Frisbee   wait in line   hold a sign
go to a rock festival   unfold a blanket   perform

1

_____

2

_____

3

_____

4

_____

5

_____

6

_____

B. Unscramble the sentences.

1

going the rest room / Gram / looked at

Greta _____.

2

fold / Gram / the blanket / saw

Greta _____.

3

listened to / sing / Greta

Gramson _____.

4

him / looking at / felt / Gramson

Gram _____.

 **Read and answer the questions.**

Rock Festival

I went to a rock festival with Greta and Gramson. We could see many people wait in line before the festival.
We watched a popular band perform.
We could hear many people shouting.
It was so cool!
Gramson looked at a girl holding a sign in front of the stage.
We could only see her back.
I felt Gramson falling in love with her.
When the girl turned around, we saw that she was a young boy!
Gramson's jaw dropped and Greta and I laughed.

popular 인기 있는   shout 소리치다   fall in love with ~에게 반하다   back 뒷모습
one's jaw drop 크게 놀라 입을 쩍 벌리다   laugh aloud 큰 소리로 웃다

1 Did the three kids watch dancers dancing?

_____

2 Who did Gramson look at in front of the stage?

_____

3 What could the three kids see before the festival?

_____

GRAM SPEAKING Look and make a story with the correct words in the sentences.

 **A**
 **B**
 **C**
 **D**

A Gram watched Greta [took] [taking] his guitar.

B And he listened to Greta [playing] [to play] the guitar.

C Suddenly Gram heard Greta [broke] [break] a string.

D Then Gram saw Greta [ran away] [running away] .

 **GRAM WRITING** Look and complete the sentences using the given hints.

1 Gram's mom _____.

Gram / go out secretly / felt

2 Greta _____.

Gram / eat pizza / saw

3 Gramson _____.

his cat / crying under the bed / heard

4 Gram _____.

his team / watched / win the game

FUNNY GRAM

Square Chess

Prepare 4 markers for each player. During your turn, move your marker on the board and make a sentence within 3 seconds. Use the given hints like "*I saw Gram laughing.*" If your sentence is correct, your marker can stay in its spot.

- barbecue sausages
- play basketball
- read a newspaper
- (Gram) wait in line

- perform
- unfold a blanket
- (Gramson) clean his room
- (Gram) hold a sign

- (rock band) sing
- (Gramson) a cat crying
- (Gram) break the window
- (Gram) play the drums

- (Gram) go shopping
- play Frisbee
- (Gram) fix his guitar
- (Gramson) go surfing
- (Greta) eat a hotdog
- (Gram) fix his guitar

- (Greta) play the guitar
- (Gramson) shout at the festival

- (Gramson) use Gram's laptop
- (Greta) look(ing) at Gram

Unit 08
Please Make Greta Set The Table

GRAM TALK Track 29 ☐ Listen ☐ Repeat ☐ Role play

Hmm… Greta, please have Gramson decorate the party room.

OK.

Gramson, please make Greta serve the food now.

OK.

Greta, can you have the movie run now?

Now? OK.

Gramson, can you get my birthday cake set on the table?

Now? OK.

Now I'm going to have my hair cut.

Still?

Don't worry, Gram.

We will finish up soon.

GRAM Expressions Track 30   **ABC** Listen and number the pictures in order. Track 31

clean up the trash

decorate the room

serve the food

blow out the candles

have one's hair cut

GRAM POINT — Sentence Structures 4: V + O + OC

Causative Verbs

- Some verbs are used to say that we arrange for somebody else to do something for us. These verbs can be used with an object followed by a base verb form or a past participle.

I	had	my sister	arrive	early.
My brother	got	his bike	repaired.	
They	let	the kids	play	in the park.

- Here are some causative verbs.

> have, make, get, let, help, keep, etc.

Ex My dad made me do my homework.
She had her son cook dinner for her.

사역동사도 지각동사처럼 목적어와 목적보어를 가지는데, 목적어가 직접 그 동작을 할 때는 "동사 원형"이 오고, 목적어가 사물이거나 수동적인 상태일 때는 "과거분사"가 온단다.

08

GRAM CHECK UP

Choose the correct words.

1 Gram's mom let Gram [went | go] to the cinema.

2 Greta had a tooth [filled | filling].

3 Gramson made Greta [turned | turn] down the TV.

 **A. Fill in the blanks and write down the meanings.**

| decorate | blow out | set |
| clean up | serve | have / cut |

1

_____ _____ the candles

→ _____

2

_____ one's hair _____

→ _____

3

_____ the room

→ _____

4

_____ _____ the trash

→ _____

5

_____ the table

→ _____

6

_____ the food

→ _____

B. Unscramble the sentences.

1   wash his car / Gramson / had

Gram's dad _____.

2   stay / Greta / after class / made

The teacher _____.

3   let / use her phone / her brother

Greta _____.

GRAM READING Track 32 **Read and answer the questions.**

Never Again Birthday Party

I had my birthday party yesterday.
Greta and Gramson helped me prepare the
party. I let them know the to-do list.
I made Gramson decorate the room.
I had Greta set the table and food.
I had them do other things for the party.
Suddenly it started to rain heavily.
So, none of my friends could come.
So we ate all the snacks and sweets.
Then, today all three of us had our teeth filled at
the dental clinic.
Because of all those sweets...

| to-do list 할일 목록 | rain heavily 비가 심하게 많이 오다 |
| have one's teeth filled 충치를 때우다(치료하다) | eat up 다 먹다 |

GRAM COMPREHENSION

1 What did Gram have Greta do?

_____

2 Why couldn't Gram's friends come to his party?

Because _____

3 Why did the three of them have their teeth filled?

Because _____

1   Q: What did Gram have Greta do?   A: Gram _____

[Greta / fix his guitar / had]

2   Q: What did Greta let Gramson do?   A: Greta _____

[let / use her phone / Gramson]

3   Q: What did Gramson make Gram   A: Gramson _____
    do after school?

[Gram / wait / after school / made]

GRAM WRITING   Look and complete the sentences using the given hints.

1      Gram's mom _____.

Gram / wash the dishes / made

2      Greta _____.

Gram / use her bike / let

3      Gramson _____.

feed his cat / Gram / had

4      Greta _____.

Gram / made / clean up the trash

Light Up The Candles!

Prepare 2 dice, a paper clip, a pencil, and two colored pencils. During your turn, roll the dice and spin the spinner. Using the subject, the verb and the phrase you got from the spinner, make a sentence within 3 seconds like "*Gram had Greta make dinner.*" If your sentence is correct, color one of the candles. The player who colors in more candles, is the winner.

Unit 09
I Enjoy Watching Cartoons

I like going to school. My friends are really fun.

Oh, you do? I hate going to school.

My friends are always busy. They love reading and studying.

I know I have to study hard like them.

But we can enjoy doing other things.

I like making model airplanes.

Right. I enjoy watching cartoons.

I love playing computer games.

I love playing soccer.

Yes, ma'am!

You two have exams tomorrow! Please stop chatting and go back to your study.

GRAM Expressions (Track 34) Listen and number the pictures in order. (Track 35)

make a model airplane

watch cartoons

take a picture

chat with

make cupcakes

play the guitar

GRAM POINT

Verb Pattern1 : Verb + ~ing

- Some verbs have an ~ing form after them. The ~ing form is used like a noun.

I	like	playing baseball.
John	hates	eating vegetables.
We	enjoy	reading books.
They	began	playing the music.

- Here are some of the verbs which take an ~ing form after them.

enjoy, like, love, begin, hate, finish, go, stop, keep

Ex I like writing stories for others.
    I finished doing my homework at 3.

동사들 중에는 "동사원형 + ing"
형태를 목적어로 취하는 동사들이
있단다. 이 동사들은 잘 기억해야 해~.
→ enjoy, like, love, begin, hate, finish,
   go, stop, keep

09

GRAM CHECK UP

Fill in the blanks using the correct forms of the given verbs.

1  Greta doesn't like _____ _____ get up
early in the morning.

2  Gramson enjoys _____ bake   cookies.

3  Gram loves _____ draw   a picture for his sister.

 **A. Write down the correct phrases from the box.**

> play the guitar   watch cartoons   make cupcakes
> make a model airplane   take a picture   chat with

1

_____

2

_____

3

_____

4

_____

5

_____

6

_____

B. Complete the sentences to find out what Gram and Gramson like, love, and hate doing.

1   go to the cinema / watch cartoons

Gram enjoys _____.

He likes _____ to the _____.

2   visit Joe's Sweets store / eat chocolate

Gramson enjoys _____.

He loves _____ chocolate.

3   study math / learn French

Gram loves _____ French.

But he hates _____.

Likes And Hates

My sister Greta likes making dresses.
But she hates trying on her dresses.
She always makes them too small.

My cousin Gramson loves writing poems.
But he hates reciting his poems.

I enjoy writing stories for others.
But I hate reading my stories to others.
Everybody has his or her own
likes and hates.

write poems 시를 쓰다 recite a poem 시를 낭송하다 own 자신의 likes 좋아하는 것들 hates 싫어하는 것들

GRAM COMPREHENSION

1 What does Greta hate?

_____

2 What does Gramson love?

_____

3 What does Gram enjoy?

_____

 **Read and complete the answers using the given hints.**

1 Q: What do you hate doing?   A: _____

[go out in the rain]

2 Q: What do you enjoy doing?   A: _____

[listen to rock music]

3 Q: What does Gram stop doing?   A: He _____

[make so much noise]

4 Q: What does Gram love doing?   A: He _____

[chat with Gramson]

 **Write what Gram enjoys, likes, loves and hates dong using the given hints.**

I enjoy
• watch cartoons
• eat chicken

I love
• play the guitar
• chat with Gramson

I like
• go in-line skating
• write stories

I hate
• take a shower
• study math

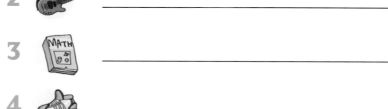

1 He enjoys watching cartoons.

2 _____.

3 _____.

4 _____.

5 _____.

6 _____.

7 _____.

8 _____.

Cupcake Factory

Prepare the verb die, a coin, and different colored pencils. During your turn, flick the coin on the board and roll the die. Make a sentence using a verb from the verb die and the hints from where your coin lands. For example: *"I enjoy listening to rock music."* If your sentence is correct, color the cupcake your coin landed on.

I Want To Do My Hair

  □ **Listen** □ **Repeat** □ **Role play**

GRAM Expressions Track 38   Listen and number the pictures in order. Track 39

get a haircut

go on a trip

go surfing

see some paintings

learn French

watch the fireworks

GRAM POINT: Verb Pattern2: Verb + To Verb Form

- Some verbs have to + base verb after them. The to + base verb is used like a noun.

I	want	to meet Gramson.
You	decided	to buy a new bike.
We	need	to get some rest.

- Here are some of the verbs which take to + base verb after them.

> want, decide, plan, hope, expect, need,
> promise, would like, learn, ask, prepare, etc.

Ex He **planned** to come back here by 3 o'clock.

We'd **like(=would like)** to go to New York this summer.

- Sometimes some verbs can take to + base verb or a base verb + ing form with almost no difference in meaning. These verbs are: **begin, hate, like, love**, etc.
Ex I like to cook. ≒ I like cooking.

동사들 중에는 "to + 기본동사"
형태를 목적어로 취하는 동사들이
있어. 중요한 거니까 잘 기억해두자.

10

Choose the correct forms of the given verbs.

1

Gram wants   eating / to eat   some hamburgers.

2

Gramson needs   to study / studied   math more.

 **A. Complete each phrase.**

learn	haircut	fireworks
surfing	paintings	go on

1 watch the _____

2 go _____

3 get a _____

4 _____ French

5 _____ _____ a trip

6 see some _____

B. Choose the correct verb to complete the sentences using to.

1  Gram forgets _____ his dog.

2  Greta decided _____ her hair style.

3  Gramson is learning _____ the drums.

4  Greta wants _____ to the Disneyland.

go
change
play
feed

Early Vacation Planning...

Gramson, Greta, and I are planning for our summer vacation.

We want to go to the mountain. We hope to go rafting. We also expect to sleep under the stars. Isn't this cool?

Greta decided to bring her tent.

Gramson is planning to build a campfire.

Our summer vacation seems just perfect!

But, I almost forgot to check one thing; before the summer starts, we must get good grades on our exams.

> go rafting 래프팅을 하러 가다   seem ～처럼 보이다
> get good grades 좋은 점수를 받다   build a campfire 모닥불을 만들다

GRAM COMPREHENSION

1 What do the three of them want to do this summer vacation?

_____

2 What did Greta decide to do for their summer vacation?

_____

3 What does Gramson plan to do for their summer vacation?

_____

 **Look and answer the questions using the given hints.**

1

What does Gram want to be?

_____

[be a painter]

2

What is Greta planning to do?

_____

[go scuba diving]

3

What does Gramson want to do?

_____

[roast hot dogs]

 **Write what Greta wants, forgets, promises, and hopes to do using the given lists.**

I want
• swim with a dolphin
• ride on a motorboat

I forget
• feed my cat
• send Gram a birthday card

I promise
• study hard
• clean my room tonight

I hope
• go to Paris this summer
• see the "Mona Lisa"

1 She often forgets to feed her cat.

2 _____.

3 _____.

4 _____.

5 _____.

6 _____.

7 _____.

8 _____.

FUNNY GRAM — Candy Tray

Each player needs a colored pencil. Take turns by playing rock, paper, scissors. During your turn, choose a candy to make a sentence using the given hints. If the sentence is correct, circle the candy.

want / go rafting

promise / send an email

I want to go rafting.

plan / go hiking

hope / visit London

need / bring my swimsuit

want / be a firefighter

learn / play the violin

expect / finish my homework

plan / go to New York

prepare / go on a picnic

prepare / take exams

decide / buy a new bike

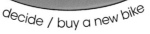

hope / speak French

Unit 11

Who Will Do The Presentation?

  ☐ **Listen**   ☐ **Repeat**   ☐ **Role play**

Hey guys! Did you hear about the school cooking contest?

No. When and where?

One month from now in the school hall.

I want to attend the contest. Can we work in groups?

Cool! So what can we make?

How about a rainbow rice cake?

Great! Who will find the recipe?

You can, Gram

Good. Then who will do the presentation?

Maybe...you can, Gram.

Then why work in a group?

As your helpers,

we can try your food.

 **Listen and number the pictures in order.**

attend the contest

do the presentation

work in groups

win a contest

try food

GRAM POINT Question Words

- Question words are used to ask questions.

"Who" is used to ask about people.	Who are you?
"Which" is used to indicate the specified people or things.	Which bag is yours?
"What" is used to find out more about people and things when there are many possible answers.	What do you want to do?
"Where" is used to ask about places.	Where's my bag?
"When" is used to ask about time.	When is your birthday?
"Why" is used to ask for a reason.	Why are you angry?
"How" is used to ask about the way to do something.	How do you make pizza?

- *What, which* and *how* can be combined with other words to form phrases that are often used as question words.

Ex What time is it?
How many cats do you have?

의문사가 있는 의문문에는 "Yes" 나 "No" 로 대답하지 않고, 그 질문에 대한 답을 말해야 돼.

11

GRAM CHECK UP
Write down the correct question words.

QUESTION WORDS	How When What Where Why Who

1 [   ] won the contest?

2 [   ] is your name?

3 [   ] is your concert?

4 [   ] are you going?

5 [   ] could you go there?

6 [   ] didn't you say so?

 **A. Fill in the blanks and write down the meanings.**

rice cake	try	win
presentation	attend	in groups

1 do the _____

➡ _____

2 _____ a contest

➡ _____

3 _____ the contest

➡ _____

4 work _____ _____

➡ _____

5 _____ food

➡ _____

6 rainbow _____ _____

➡ _____

B. Choose the correct question words and answer the questions using the given hints.

1 Who / Which likes rice cakes?

Gramson _____.   rice cakes / likes

2 Who / Whose laptop is this?

This _____.   is / Gram's laptop

3 What / How did Greta get good scores?

Greta _____.   hard / studied

 **RAM READING** **Read and answer the questions.**

Cooking Contest Registration

✳ Fill in the blanks and answer the questions to complete the form.

Team Name	Gram Geeks	E-mail: gramgeek@grammar.net
Contestants	1. Gramson, Brad	M. P. : 080-3333-2222
	2. Gram, Lee	Presentation Being ready YES ☑ NO ☐
	3. Greta, Lee	Entry Category: desserts

✳ What is your dish?

Rainbow Rice Cake

✳ Where did you find your recipe?

On the internet and from a Korean cook book.

✳ Why did you choose this dish?

We wanted to show a healthy Korean traditional dessert.

✳ How can you make your dish?

Please check the second file for the recipe.

✳ Which ingredients did you use? (3-4 ingredients)

Rice flour, autumn squash, purple sweet potato, raison.

recipe 레시피, 요리방법
rice flour 쌀가루
autumn squash 단호박
mainly 주로
purple sweet potato 자색 고구마
raison 건포도
dessert 디저트
dish 음식

11

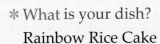  **RAM COMPREHENSION**

1 What was Gram Geeks' dish?

_____

2 Where did Gram Geeks find their recipe?

They found their recipe _____

3 Why did Gram Geeks choose this dish?

They wanted to _____

GRAM SPEAKING

Look at the pictures and fill in the blanks.

A

B

C

D

A _____ did Greta _____ information for making the rice cake?

➡ She collected data _____.

B _____ did the kids _____ for the contest?

➡ They prepared at _____ house.

C _____ helped them prepare the contest?

➡ _____ helped them prepare for it.

D _____ much rice flour did Gram use?

➡ Gram used two _____ of rice flour.

GRAM WRITING

Write an email inviting Gramson's friend to the school cooking contest using the given expressions.

how   contest   when   attend   where   What

Hi Sally,

Our school cooking _____ is on Saturday.

I decided to _____ the contest with Greta and Gram.

_____ is my team name? Our team name is "Gram Geeks".

It's fun, right? We will make "Rainbow rice cake".

Please come and enjoy the contest.

Oh, Sally, _____ is your piano contest? _____ is the contest and _____ can I get there?

Please let me know. We will go to your piano contest, too. See you then.

Gramson,

FUNNY GRAM

Sweet Mini Pie Time

Cut out and prepare the question word die and the 14 mini pie cards. Give 7 mini pie cards to each player. During your turn, roll the die and choose a picture on the tray. Using the hints from the die and the picture, make a question within 3 seconds like "**Who cleaned up the trash?**" If your question is right, then cover up the picture on the tray using one of your pie cards. The first one to cover 7 pictures with his or her pie cards, is the winner.

clean up the trash

do a presentation

see some paintings

play Frisbee

decorate the party

play the guitar

serve the food

learn French

work in groups

win the contest

go to the rock festival

try food

watch cartoons

11

If You Don't Hurry Up...

GRAM TALK Track 45 □ Listen □ Repeat □ Role play

Gram, if you don't mow the lawn, you won't get any pocket money.

Gram, if you watch TV too closely, you will have bad eye sight.

Gram, if you eat too much, you will feel very ill.

Where are my books?

Gram, if you don't tidy your room, you won't find your books.

Oh, I'm running out of time!

Gram, if you don't finish your homework like this, you will get bad grades.

If you don't hurry up,

we will miss the movie!

GRAM Expressions Track 46 Listen and number the pictures in order. Track 47

tidy her room

get bad grades

have bad eye sight

get pocket money

feel ill

mow the lawn

G RAM POINT   First Conditionals: If

- Conditional sentences are to talk about the future. They have two phrases.
  The basic pattern is "If + S + present tense ~, S + will (not) + V~."

If-Phrase			will / won't (=will not) -Phrase		
If	she	finds out,	she	will	be angry with you.
If	we	don't hurry up,	we	won't	get there in time.
If	it	rains tomorrow,	I	won't	go out.

- Put a comma (,) in the middle of the sentence when the *if-phrase* comes **first**. You don't need a comma when it comes second.

Ex   If it's sunny tomorrow, we'll have a picnic.
    = We'll have a picnic if it's sunny tomorrow.

"If 조건문" 에서는 "If" 가 포함된 쪽은 "현재시제" 를 나머지 구문에서는 "미래" 시제가 사용된다는 점을 잊지 말자.

 G RAM CHECK UP   Circle the *if-phrase* and underline the *will/won't-phrase* in each sentence.

1 If Gram tells it to the teacher, I will be in trouble.

2 You will get very cold if you go out in the rain.

3 I will show you my CDs if you come to my house.

4 If we win the contest, I'll have a party.

A. Write down the correct phrases.

| get pocket money | feel ill | mow the lawn |
| have bad eye sight | tidy her room | get bad grades |

1

_____

2

_____

3

_____

4

_____

5

_____

6

_____

B. Complete the sentences using *will* or *won't*.

1   If it rains tomorrow,

we _____.

    go to the beach

2   If you help me make cookies,

we _____.

    together / eat cookies

3   If you practice playing the piano a lot,

you _____.

    be a pianist

G RAM READING
Track 48

Read and answer the questions.

Instead Of My Family

My bike is too old so I want a new one.
To buy my new bike, I'm planning to make
some pocket money for it.
If I mow the lawn on Mondays,
and if I wash the dishes on Tuesdays,
and if I fix my cousin Gramson's model robot
on Wednesdays, and if I do the laundry
on Thursdays, and if I take out the trash
on Fridays, and if I wash my dad's car on Saturdays,
and if I water the plants on Sundays, then I will get 6,000
won per week!

Isn't this great?
This is a perfect plan!

- Mow the lawn: ₩1,500
- Wash the dishes: ₩500
- Fix Gramson's model robot: ₩1,000
- Do the laundry: ₩500
- Take out the trash: ₩500
- Wash dad's car: ₩1,500
- Water the plants: ₩500

| instead of ~ 대신에 | fix 수리하다 | do the laundry 세탁하다 |
| take out the trash 쓰레기를 버리다 | per week (1)주마다 |

G RAM COMPREHENSION

1 Why does Gram want to make some pocket money?

Gram _____.

2 How much will Gram get if he takes out the trash?

If Gram _____ , _____.

3 How much will Gram get if he works instead of his family per week?

If Gram _____ , _____.

12

 **SPEAKING** Read and complete the answers using the given hints.

1 Q: If it is sunny tomorrow, Gram and Greta will go in-line skating.

What will they do if it is sunny?

go in-line skating / sunny

A: If _____ tomorrow, they _____.

2 Q: If Gram helps Greta do homework, Greta will buy him ice cream.

What will Greta do if Gram helps her?

help / Gram / ice cream / buy

A: Greta _____ if Gram _____ her do homework.

3 Q: If it rains tomorrow, Gramson will watch a video at home.

What will Gramson do if it rains?

rain / a video / watch

A: If _____ tomorrow, Gramson will _____ at home.

GRAM WRITING Match the phrases, then write five sentences. One is done for you.

1. miss the bus	pass the exam
2. study hard	get sunburned
3. lie in the sun	not learn anything
4. touch something hot	be late for the movie
5. eat too much	burn yourself
6. don't listen in class	get fat

1 If you miss the bus, you will be late for the movie.

2 _____.

3 _____.

4 _____.

5 _____.

6 _____.

Make Some Pocket Money!

Prepare the 10 pieces of 500 won coins and 8 pieces of 1000 won paper money. Shuffle the 15 If-Phrase cards and place them on the table facing down. During your turn, take one of the If-Phrase cards and read it aloud. If you find its matching picture and make a full If-sentence within 5 seconds, you will get the money marked on the picture. If you can't make a sentence, put the If-Phrase card back in the stack. The player with the most money is the winner.

buy a new bike

get wet

get sunburned

be late for school

have bad eye sight

get bad marks

go on a picnic

not get better

get a toothache

not find your books

get pocket money

get fat

watch a video

miss the movie

be a pianist

I Am As Tall As Steve

Who is the boy in the picture?

He is my friend, Steve.

Oh, he is cool.

Look at me. I am as tall as Steve.

Are you as strong as Steve?

Yes, I am as strong as Steve.

Are you as smart as Steve?

Of course. I am as smart as Steve.

But… sometimes I am not as smart as Steve.

GRAM Expressions Track 50 ABC Listen and number the pictures in order. Track 51

 strong

shy

smart

talkative

friendly

popular

GRAM POINT As ~ As / Not As ~ As

- We use as + adjective/adverb + as to show that two people, places, or things are the same.

			Adjective/Adverb			
I	am		old			you.
Anne	is	as	kind	as		James.
I	study		hard			Mike.
Derek	speaks		slowly			Wendy.

- We use not to make negative sentences.

Ex Mary is 11 years old. Andy is 13 years old.
→ Mary is not as old as Andy.
    Daniel doesn't speak as fast as Alice.

'(not) as+형용사/부사as' 는
'~만큼 ~하다(~하지 않다)' 는 뜻이야.
'as' 와 'as' 사이에는 형용사나
부사가 온다는 것을 기억하자!

GRAM CHECK UP

Look and complete the sentences using *(not) as...as* and the given words.

1

Greta is _____ Gramson.
popular

2

Gram is _____ Gramson.
old

3

Greta runs _____ Gram.
fast

4

Gram is _____ Greta.
strong

RAM PRACTICE **A. Write the correct adjectives starting with the given letters.**

1

s_____

2

f_____

3

s_____

4

t_____

5

s_____

6

p_____

B. Read and answer the questions using (not) as…as.

1 A: Is Greta strong?

B: Yes. She _____ Gram.

2 A: Does Gramson sing well?

B: Yes. He _____ Greta.

3 A: Is Gram tall?

B: No. He _____ Gramson.

4 A: Does Greta jump high?

B: Yes. She _____ Gram.

5 A: Is Gramson friendly?

B: Yes. He _____ Steve.

6 A: Does Gram get up early?

B: No. He _____ Gramson.

Best Friends

I'm Gram and my cousin is Gramson.
We look a lot different.
I'm 12 and he is 15.
I'm 5 feet tall but I'm not as tall as him.
He's 6 feet tall.
Also I'm very talkative, so Gramson is not as talkative as me. He is quiet.
But we have one thing in common.
We both like cartoons.
I like cartoons as much as Gramson does.
That's why we can be best friends.

have in common 공통점이 있다	different 다른	best friend 가장 친한 친구

1 Is Gramson as old as Gram?

_____

2 Is Gram as tall as Gramson?

_____

3 Does Gram like cartoons as much as Gramson does?

_____

 **Answer the questions using the given information.**

1

Is Greta tall?

_____

not as ~ as / her mom

2

Is Greta popular?

_____

as ~ as / Gramson

3

Does Greta run fast?

_____

not as ~ as / Gram

 **Write a descriptive sentence using the given hints.**

1

as hard as / study / Steve

Gram _____.

2

as well as / Gramson / play the guitar

Gram _____.

3

as strong as / not / his dad / is

Gram _____.

Twenty Questions

One player looks and selects one of the cards but does not tell anyone. The other player asks a Yes or No question. He or she has only 20 questions to guess which card was selected.

strong
thin

shy
smart

short
strong

Is he strong?

fat
weak

tall
talkative

short
fat

Yes! He is
as strong as you.

fat
smart

thin
friendly

shy
thin

No! He is not
as strong as you.

Which One Is Faster?

Unit 14

GRAM TALK

Track 53 □ Listen □ Repeat □ Role play

Are you ready? Which one is shorter?

It's in your right hand.

Sorry, Greta. You're wrong. Give me one.

Here it is.

Then which one is faster?

It's in your... left hand.

Wrong! Give me two.

OK. Here you are.

Yoo-hoo! Are you ready again? Which one is higher?

Hmm... In your right hand!

Yes, I'm right! Wow, I got a bonus. Give up all your cards, Gram!

Oh, my!

GRAM Expressions

Track 54 ABC Listen and number the pictures in order. Track 55

fast – slow | expensive – cheap | fat – thin | young – old | hungry – full | high - low

- Comparative **adjectives** are to talk about the difference between two people, places, or things.
We add –er or more to form the comparative form.

–er	1 syllable	old – older large - larger * big – bigger hot – hotter thin – thinner
	2 syllables: -y ➜ -i + -er	busy – busier easy - easier happy – happier pretty - prettier
more	2 and more syllables	famous – more famous useful – more useful interesting – more interesting
Irregular Forms		good/well – better bad – worse many/much – more

비교급은 '~보다 더 ~한' 의 뜻으로 둘 이상의 사람이나 사물을 비교할 때 쓰는 말이야. 보통 끝에 –er을 붙이지만, 형태가 다른 것도 있으니 잘 기억해야 해.

- The word than comes after the comparative adjective.
Ex A bicycle is cheaper than a car.

- We use the subject pronoun after *than*. We can use the verb as well.
Ex I am older than **she is.** / I run faster than **he does.**

 GRAM CHECK UP Circle the correct comparatives in sentences.

1

I'm   nicier / nicer   than you. Everybody loves me.

 2

I'm   smarter / smartter   than you and
I'm   intelligenter / more intelligent   than you.

 **A. Unscramble the words and write in the letter that matches the picture.**

① evienxeps

② guoyn

③ rnhygu

④ ghhi

⑤ ntih

⑥ wsol

⑦ aphec

⑧ lufl

B. Correct the mistakes in red and rewrite the sentences.

1 We arrived early than Susie.

➡ _____.

2 Amy drives carefully than Steven.

➡ _____.

3 The train is good than the bus in many ways.

➡ _____.

4 Traveling by an airplane is more quick than a car.

➡ _____.

GRAM READING

Track 56

Read the story and answer the questions.

We Will Go To Gyeongju By Bus

This weekend my family will go to Gyeongju.
My dad's car is more comfortable than a bus.
However, we will take an express bus.
Why? It is faster than driving.
There will be more cars on the road this
weekend. However, the bus uses the bus lane
and it takes only four hours.
Taking a bus is also cheaper than driving.
I can't wait for the trip.

express bus 고속버스	road 도로	weekend 주말	lane 차로
take (시간이) 걸리다	wait for ~을 기다리다	comfortable 편안한	

GRAM COMPREHENSION

14

1 Where will the girl's family go this weekend?

_____

2 Why will the girl's family take an express bus?

_____

3 Is taking a bus more expensive than driving?

_____

 **Look and answer the questions using the given hints.**

16 yrs   10 yrs   10 yrs   16 yrs

Kevin   Jihun   Ben   Chris

1 Q: Is Jihun taller than Chris?

   A: No, _____. Jihun _____ Chris.   short

2 Q: Is Ben thinner than Kevin?

   A: No, _____. Ben _____ Kevin.   fat

3 Q: Is Kevin stronger than Jihun?

   A: No, _____. Kevin _____ Jihun.   weak

 **Look and complete the sentences using the given hints.**

The family didn't have much time for the train.
They took a taxi.
The taxi stopped at many traffic lights.

HINTS
was slower than
arrived late
was more expensive

1 It _____ the subway.

2 It _____ than the subway.

3 Unfortunately, they _____ for the train.

Funny Gram

Crossword Puzzle

Complete the puzzle.

Across:
① c _ m _ o _ _ _ l e
② _ _ _ _ _ _ _
③ _ _ _ _ e
④ f _ _ _ _
⑤ l / e
⑥ c _ e _ _ _ _

ACROSS

1. The car is usually more _____ than a bus.
2. I arrived _____ than Minho.
3. Traveling by a bus is _____ than a car.
4. An airplane is _____ than a car.
5. Taking a bus is _____ than driving.

DOWN

1. A train is _____ than a bus.
2. A bicycle is _____ than a motorcycle.
3. Wearing a helmet is _____ than no helmet.
4. The taxi fare is more _____ than the bus fare.
5. We arrived _____ than Mike.

Unit 15 What Is The Tallest Tower?

Hello and welcome to the Speed Quiz Show. Are you ready?

First. Which one of these is the oldest building?

The pyramid is the oldest!

① ② ③

Right! You got one point, Gramson.

Second. Which one of these is the tallest tower?

The CN tower is the tallest!

① ② ③

Great, Gramson. Hello, Gram. Can you hear me?

Yes, I'm just warming up!

This is the last one. Who is the most famous singer...?

Gram! Gram!

I am the most famous singer!

GRAM Expressions Track 58 ABC Listen and number the pictures in order. Track 59

hot - cold   old - new   wide - narrow   tall - short   heavy - light   famous

- Superlative **adjectives** are used to talk about the difference among three or more people, places, or things.
  We add - est or most to form the superlative form.

–est	1 syllable	great - greatest slow – slowest * big – biggest	old – oldest fast – fastest hot – hottest
	2 syllables: -y ➔ -i + -est	busy – busiest happy – happiest	easy - easiest pretty - prettiest
most	2 and more syllables	famous – most famous expensive – most expensive	popular – most popular important – most important
Irregular Forms		good/well – better bad – worst many/much – most	

- The word the comes before the superlative adjective.
  Ex Michelangelo is the greatest artist of all time.
  Beethoven is the most popular composer
  in the world.

최상급은 '~중에서 가장 ~한' 의 뜻으로, 셋
이상의 사람, 장소, 사물을 비교할 때 사용해.
형용사 뒤에 '-est' 를 붙이거나, 형용사 앞에
'most' 를 붙이면 되는데, 최상급 앞에는 반드시
'the' 가 온다는 점도 기억하자!

GRAM **CHECK UP**   Circle the correct superlatives in sentences.

1

Who's the fattest / fatest amongst us? Is it you?

2

What? I have no idea but I think I'm the

most smart / smartest and the

most prettiest / prettiest of us.

A. Fill in the blanks to complete the words and write in the letter that matches the picture.

a b c d
e f g h

① na____ro____ ◯   ② ____ ____a____y ◯

③ f____ m____ ____s ◯   ④ ____i____e ◯

⑤ l__ g____ ____ ◯   ⑥ ____ol____ ◯

⑦ ____a____l ◯   ⑧ o____ ____ ◯

B. Write the correct names or superlatives of the given adjectives.

1 Brad is _____ boy.   old

2 Ken has _____ hair.   long

3 Andy is _____ boy.   smart

4 _____ has the shortest hair.

5 David is _____ and
_____ boy.   young / fat

16 yrs  17 yrs

Ken   **Brad**

14 yrs  8 yrs

Andy   **David**

GRAM READING
Track 60
Read the story and answer the questions.

Vincent van Gogh

I went to the National Art Museum last
Saturday.
There was a special exhibition.
It was the biggest Vincent van Gogh
exhibition.
He didn't live a happy life, but he
painted some of the most famous
paintings in the world.
He is one of the greatest painters
in history.
He is my favorite artist, too.
I was very happy to see Sunflowers,
his most popular painting.

---

national 국가의   special 특별한   exhibition 전시회   favorite 가장 좋아하는

GRAM COMPREHENSION

1 Where did the boy go last weekend?

_____

2 Is Vincent van Gogh a great painter?

_____

3 What painting did the boy see?

_____

15

GRAM SPEAKING Look and make a story with the given expressions.

what / the longest / the oldest / The widest river

Gramson, Greta and I were talking about some of the world's best rivers.

A Gram said, "_____ is the Amazon river, right?"

B Gramson said, "Right. But it's not _____ one."

C Greta said, "Really? Then _____ is the longest?"

Gramson said, "The Nile is the longest."

D Gram said, "And it's one of _____ rivers, too."

GRAM WRITING Complete the sentences using an adjective from Box A and a phrase from Box B. Change the adjectives to superlatives.

A	B
narrow	in the world
expensive	of all the sea animals
hot	in my town
heavy	on the test
good	in the store
difficult	in California

1 Question 3 was *the most difficult* question *on the test*.

2 Gram bought _____ sneakers _____.

3 The Death Valley in California is _____ place _____.

4 This road is _____ road _____.

5 Yuna Kim is _____ figure skater _____.

6 The blue whale is _____ animal _____.

Hidden Word

Look at the pictures and fill in the word puzzle using the superlatives. Then, write the hidden word in the blank.

① shy

② proud

happy ③

④ cold

dry ⑤

slow ⑥

⑦ fat

⑧ thin

⑨ mild

⑩ heavy

⑪ angry

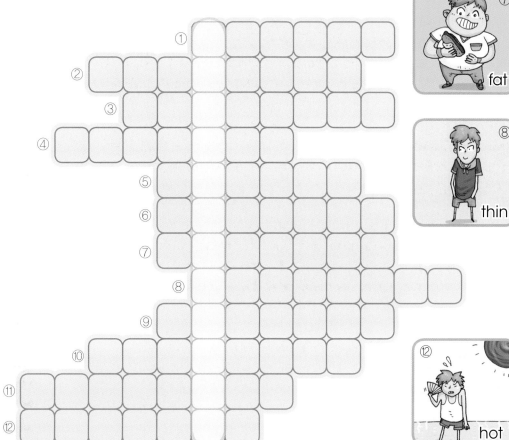

The hidden word is _____.

Have You Ever Cooked A Turkey?

GRAM TALK Track 61 ☐ Listen ☐ Repeat ☐ Role play

Gram, Gramson! Help me, please. It's about Thanksgiving dinner.

What can we do for you?

OK.

Gram, have you ever baked a pumpkin pie?

PUMPKIN PIE

Uh....no.

OK. Gramson, have you ever popped Indian popcorn?

POP CORN

Indian popcorn? Well…no.

Fine. Gram, have you ever cooked a turkey?

That huge turkey, you mean? No.

Come on! Then what have you ever done for Thanksgiving Day?

We've eaten a lot of turkey...

...every Thanksgiving Day.

GRAM Expressions Track 62 ABC Listen and number the pictures in order. Track 63

pop Indian popcorn

bake a pumpkin pie

cook a turkey

peel potatoes

keep a diary

eat with chopsticks

GRAM POINT Have (Has) + P.P

- When we talk about some experiences that have happened during your life up to now, we can express them using the "have(has) + past participle" form. In this case, you can use **ever** in questions and **never** in negative sentences.

Have	you	ever	played	the flute?
Has	Sam		been	to New York?

→ Answer: <u>Yes, I have</u>. or <u>No, I haven't</u>.

I	have	never	played	the flute.
Sam	has		been	to New York.

- We use "have(has) not + past particle" to express the negative sentences.
  Ex He hasn't been (= has not) to France.

- Here is a list of some regular past particles. Most verbs have an ending in –ed.

Base Verb	Past Simple	Past Particle
open	opened	opened
carry	carried	carried

- However some past particles are not so easy. Here is a list of some irregular past particles.

> "~(한) 적이 있다"라고 말할 때, "have + 과거분사(p.p.)"의 형태를 사용하는데, 좀 더 의미를 강조하여 물어보는 문장에서는 "ever"를, 부정으로 말할 때는 "never"를 사용해. 그리고 과거분사형은 잘 외워두도록 하자.

Base Verb	Past Simple	Past Particle	Base Verb	Past Simple	Past Particle
am / is / are	was / were	been	go	went	gone
meet	met	met	buy	bought	bought
bring	brought	brought	come	came	come
drink	drank	drunk	eat	ate	eaten
forget	forgot	forgotten	have	had	had
give	gave	given	keep	kept	kept
know	knew	known	leave	left	left
make	made	made	say	said	said
run	ran	run	send	sent	sent
see	saw	seen	sit	sat	sat
sing	sang	sung	speak	spoke	spoken
swim	swam	swum	take	took	taken
think	thought	thought	write	wrote	written

A. Fill in the blanks and write down each meaning.

| turkey | bake | with |
| pop | keep | peel |

1

cook a _____

→ _____

2

_____ a pumpkin pie

→ _____

3

eat _____ chopsticks

→ _____

4

_____ Indian popcorn

→ _____

5

_____ a diary

→ _____

6

_____ potatoes

→ _____

B. Choose the correct past particles.

1

Gram has [helpped] [helped] Greta.

2

Gramson has [drunk] [drank] a carton of milk.

3

Greta has [being] [been] to Paris.

4

Gram has [eaten] [ate] sushi.

What We've Never Done

Have you ever thought about what you've never done?
Gram's never baked a pie.
He's never kept a diary.
Gramson has never cleaned his room.
He's never eaten with chopsticks.

And what about me?
I've never been late for school.
I've never forgotten my brother's birthday.
I've never talked behind my brother's back.
Yes, I always talk to him openly.

forget 잊어버리다   talk behind somebody's back 뒷담화를 하다

GRAM COMPREHENSION

1 Has Gram ever kept a diary?

_____

2 Has Gramson ever cleaned his room?

_____

3 Has Greta ever forgotten her brother's birthday?

_____

 **Look and write down the answers and write down the numbers that match the pictures.**

A  B  C  D

1 Q: Where has Greta been?

A: Greta _____. London / has been to ◯

2 Q: Has Gram ever cooked a turkey?

A: No, _____. ◯

3 Q: Has Gramson ever popped Indian popcorn?

A: Yes, _____. ◯

4 Q: Who has read Hamlet?

A: Gram _____. Hamlet / has read ◯

 **Complete an email invitation by writing down the correct words.**

Hi Sujin,

_____ (Have) you ever _____ (be) to Thanksgiving dinner party?

Our family will have a party tomorrow.

We have never _____ (prepare) a party by ourselves.

I've never _____ (bake) a pumpkin pie.

But today I tried to bake one.

Gram _____ (have) never _____ (peel) potatoes but he did it for the party.

I also invited James and some other friends, too.

I hope you will join the party.

Greta

Thanksgiving Dinner

Prepare the Ever/Never die and 6 markers for each player.
During your turn, roll the die and choose one plate from the table.
With the given hints make a sentence within 3 seconds using "have
+ past participle" like *I've never been to Mars.* Use "Ever" for the
questions and "Never" for the negative sentences.
 If your sentence is correct, cover the plate with one of your markers.

[FUNNY GRAM EXP]
- bake a pumpkin pie
- be to London
- be to Paris
- cook a turkey
- drink a carton of milk
- eat with chopsticks
- forget one's friends
- birthdays
- have sushi
- learn Chinese
- read Hamlet
- keep one's diary
- meet a film star
- peel potatoes
- play board games
- pop Indian corn

cooked

forgotten

drunk

baked

had

popped

peeled

read

played

met

eaten

kept

been

learned

been

16

Audio Script

GRAM GRAM PLUS Book4

[Track 1] p.8

Unit 01. I Want Some Cheese

Listen to the dialogue.

Gram: Mom, do we have any bread?
Mom: No, we don't.
Gram: Then, do we have any cheese?
Mom: No.
Gram: Do we have any eggs?
Mom: Sorry. We don't have any eggs.
Gram: Then what do we have?
Mom: We have many things to buy!

[Track 2]
[GRAM Expressions]
Listen and repeat.
vegetables
fruits
seafood
dairy products
beverages
meat

[Track 03]
Listen and number the pictures in order.
1. seafood
2. beverages
3. fruits
4. dairy products
5. meat
6. vegetables

[Track 04] p.11
[GRAM READING]
Listen to the story and answer the questions.

- Let's Go Grocery Shopping! -
Dad and I are going to make chicken curry for Mom. We are making a shopping list.
First, we need some chicken.
Second, we need some carrots and potatoes.
Then, we need some mushrooms, too.
We have some onions in the refrigerator, so we don't need any more onions.
Oh, Mom loves broccoli, so we need some broccoli, too.
Let's go shopping, Dad.

[Track 05] p.14

Unit 02. He Drinks A Lot Of Water

Listen to the dialogue.

Greta: What are you drinking?
Gram: I'm drinking water.
Greta: Do you drink much water?
Gram: Yes. I drink a lot of water.
Greta: How much water do you drink a day?
Gram: I drink ten bottles of water a day.
Greta: Are you okay?
Gram: No, I'm not.
Gram: Sometimes, drinking too much water is not good for me.

[Track 06]
[GRAM Expressions]
Listen and repeat.
nuts
junk food
sweets
rice & soup
coffee & tea
steak & salad

[Track 07]
Listen and number the pictures in order.
1. sweets
2. coffee & tea
3. nuts
4. steak & salad
5. rice & soup
6. junk food

[Track 08] p.17
[GRAM READING]
Listen to the story and answer the questions.
- Let's Eat A Balanced Diet! -
We should eat a balanced diet for our health.
We should eat a lot of fresh fruits and vegetables every day.
They have a lot of vitamins and minerals.
However, we should not eat too much junk food like hamburgers, pizza, and fried chicken.
Junk food has too many calories and too much fat.
Junk food has a lot of salt, too.
Eat a balanced diet and keep healthy.

[Track 09] p.20

Unit 03. He Speaks English Well

Listen to the dialogue.
Greta: Does Jason speak English well?
Gram: Yes, he does.
Gram: He studies hard.
Greta: Does he solve math problems well?
Gram: Yes, he does.
Greta: How about you, Gram?
Gram: No, I don't.
Gram: But I eat really fast!

[Track 10]

[GRAM Expressions]

Listen and repeat.

speak English

explain

raise a hand

sit down

solve a problem

take notes

[Track 11]

Listen and number the pictures in order.

1. raise a hand

2. take notes

3. speak English

4. explain

5. sit down

6. solve a problem

[Track 12] p.23

[GRAM READING]

Listen to the story and answer the questions.

- Rules For The Test! -

Take your seat quickly and listen carefully.

Pass out the tests quickly.

When you have a question, please raise your hand quietly.

Don't talk loudly with your classmates.

Read and answer the questions carefully.

After the test, leave the classroom quietly.

[Track 13] p.26

Unit 04. I Always Walk To School

Listen to the dialogue.

Gramson: I always get up at 7.

Gram: Really? I never get up at 7.

Gram: It's too early for me.

Gramson: I usually do my homework after school.

Gramson: How about you, Gram?

Gram: I usually do my homework in the morning.

Gramson: I sometimes read books before bedtime.

Gram: Oh, you too? I always read books before bedtime like you.

[Track 14]

[GRAM Expressions]

Listen and repeat.

get up

take a shower

have breakfast

pack a schoolbag

do homework

go to bed

[Track 15]

Listen and number the pictures in order.

1. pack a schoolbag

2. take a shower

3. go to bed

4. have breakfast

5. get up

6. do homework

[Track 16] p.29

[GRAM READING]

Listen to the story and answer the questions.

- I Am An Early Bird. -

I always get up early.

I usually take a shower in the morning.

After breakfast, I always walk to school.

I am never late for school.

After school, I always do my homework first.

Then I often play with my friends or read books.

I always have dinner with my family.

After dinner, I seldom watch TV.

I always go to bed before 10 o'clock.

[Track 17] p.32

Unit 05. I Am Milking A Cow!

Listen to the dialogue

Gram: Greta, can you help me?

Greta: What do you need?

Gram: I'm milking a cow and gathering eggs.

Greta: At the same time?

Gramson: Help! Is anybody here?

Greta: What do you need?

Gramson: I'm shearing sheep and feeding a baby pig.

Greta: At the same time?

Gram: Oh, my! I'm dropping the eggs!

Greta: Oh, dear. I'll help you now.

Gramson: Please! The sheep is running away!

Greta: Oh, dear. I'll help you now.

Gram: Oh, my! All the eggs are breaking!

Gramson: My pig ran away, too!

Greta: What a mess!

[Track 18]

[GRAM Expressions]

Listen and repeat.

feed a calf

shear sheep

milk a cow

unload a truck

pick apples

gather eggs

[Track 19]

Listen and number the pictures in order.

1. milk a cow
2. pick apples
3. shear sheep
4. gather eggs
5. unload a truck
6. feed a calf

[Track 20] p.35
[GRAM READING]
Listen to the story and answer the questions.
- Love you, Grandpa! -
My grandfather has a huge farm.
Today Gramson and I helped him on his farm.
We were milking a cow.
Suddenly a big goose surprised Gramson.
He was so shocked he kicked the egg basket by mistake. All the eggs broke.
Then the basket fell on the milk bottle.
Then the milk bottle rolled into the pigpen.
And all the pigs ran away.
What a mess!
But grandfather just hugged us smiling,
"It's OK, guys. I still love you very much."
"We love you too, Grandpa!"

[Track 21] p.38
Unit 06. My Friends Sent Me Presents

Listen to the dialogue.
Greta: Wow, what are these?
Gram: Birthday presents. My friends sent me presents. You know yesterday was my birthday.
Greta: Hmm... strange. I thought your birthday is...
Gram: Greta, can I show you my presents?
Gram: A CD and a T-shirt and sneakers, and a comic book, and a...
Mailman: (Knock, knock, knock) Is anyone there?
Mailman: Oh, hi, guys. I gave you the wrong parcels yesterday. They are all for the 'School Bazaar'. Can you give them back?
Greta: Yes, here they are.
Gram: Oh, my!

[Track 22]
[GRAM Expressions]
give Greta a CD
lend Gramson his sneakers
bring the boy a T-shirt
sell the girl his photos
show Greta a model robot
pass Gram the comic books

[Track 23]
Listen and number the pictures in order.
1. pass Gram the comic books
2, sell the girl his photos
3. give Greta a CD
4. show Greta a model robot
5. lend Gramson his sneakers
6. bring the boy a T-shirt

[Track 24] p.41
[GRAM READING]
Listen to the story and answer the questions.
- At The School Bazaar -
We had a 'School Bazaar' yesterday.
Many students brought their teachers some old and new things.
Greta brought her teacher a pink T-shirt.
I brought my teacher a brand-new backpack.
A teacher taught us how to sell our things.
And the bazaar opened.
Many students near my school came.

Gramson sold a boy his model robot first.
Gramson and I showed the students Taekwondo performances, too.
It was great time to learn how to share and help each other.

[Track 25] p.44
Unit 07. Look At That Guy Playing The Guitar

Listen to the dialogue.
Gram: Can you hear the rock singer singing?
Gramson: Yes. Wow! Look at that guy playing the guitar. Awesome!
Gram: Did you bring the sign board, Gramson?
Gramson: Ta-da! Here it is.
Greta: By the way, Gram. Where is the blanket? I saw you folding the blanket this morning.
Gram: Oh, sorry, I forgot it.
Gramson: It's OK. I saw a man barbecuing over there. Can we have some hotdogs?
Gram: Great! I love hotdogs!
Greta: Alright! But we have to wait in line.
Security Guard: Please give me your tickets.
Gram: Sure, here you are.
Security Guard: Oh, these are all for the flower festival.
Gramson & Greta: What? Oh, Gram!

[Track 26]
[GRAM Expressions]
play Frisbee
wait in line
hold a sign
go to a rock festival
unfold a blanket
perform

[Track 27]

Listen and number the pictures in order.

1. perform
2. play Frisbee
3. unfold a blanket
4. wait in line
5. hold a sign
6. go to a rock festival

[Track 28] p.47

[GRAM READING]

Listen to the story and answer the questions.

- Rock Festival -

I went to a rock festival with Greta and Gramson. We could see many people wait in line before the festival.
We watched a popular band perform.
We could hear many people shouting.
It was so cool!
Gramson looked at a girl holding a sign in front of the stage. We could only see her back.
I felt Gramson falling in love with her.
When the girl turned around, we saw that she was a young boy!
Gramson's jaw dropped and Greta and I laughed.

[Track 29] p.50

Unit 08. Please Make Greta Set The Table

Listen to the dialogue.

Gram: Hmm… Greta, please have Gramson decorate the party room.
Greta: OK.
Gram: Gramson, please make Greta serve the food now.
Gramson: OK.
Gram: Greta, can you have the movie run now?

Greta: Now? OK.
Gram: Gramson, can you get my birthday cake set on the table?
Gramson: Now? OK.
Gram: Now I'm going to have my hair cut.
Gram: Still?
Gramson: Don't worry, Gram
Greta: We'll finish up soon.

[Track 30]

[GRAM Expressions]

clean up the trash
decorate the room
serve the food
blow out the candles
have one's hair cut

[Track 31]

Listen and number the pictures in order.

1. blow out the candles
2. decorate the room
3. clean up the trash
4. serve the food
5. have one's hair cut

[Track 32] p. 53

[GRAM READING]

Listen to the story and answer the questions.

- Never Again Birthday Party -

I had my birthday party yesterday.
Greta and Gramson helped me prepare the party. I let them know the to-do list.
I made Gramson decorate the room.
I had Greta set the table and food.
I had them do other things for the party.
Suddenly it started to rain heavily.
So, none of my friends could come.
So we ate all the snacks and sweets.
Then, today all three of us had our teeth filled at the dental clinic. Because of all those sweets.

[Track 33] p. 56

Unit 09. I Enjoy Watching Cartoons

Listen to the dialogue.

Gram: I like going to school. My friends are really fun.
Gramson: Oh, you do? I hate going to school.
Gramson: My friends are always busy. They love reading and studying.
Gramson: I know I have to study hard like them.
Gram: But we can enjoy doing other things.
Gramson: Right. I enjoy watching cartoons.
Gram: I like making model airplanes.
Gramson: I love playing computer games.
Gram: I love playing soccer.
Mom: You two have exams tomorrow! Please stop chatting and go back to your study.
Gram & Gramson: Yes, ma'am!

[Track 34]

[GRAM Expressions]

Listen and repeat.

make a model airplane
watch cartoons
take a picture
chat with
make cupcakes
play the guitar

[Track 35]

Listen and number the pictures in order.

1. make cupcakes
2. make a model airplane
3. chat with
4. watch cartoons
5. take a picture
6. play the guitar

[Track 36] p. 59
[GRAM READING]

Listen to the story and answer the questions.

- Likes And Hates -

My sister Greta likes making dresses.
But she hates trying on her dresses.
She always makes them too small.
My cousin Gramson loves writing poems.
But he hates reciting his poems.
I enjoy writing stories for others.
But I hate reading my stories to others.
Everybody has his or her own likes and hates.

[Track 37] p.62

Unit 10. I Want To Do My Hair

Listen to the dialogue.

Gram: Greta, where did you decide to go this summer?
Greta: I decided to go to Paris!
Gram: Wow, great! Where do you want to visit first?
Greta: I hope to visit the Eiffel tower in Paris first.
Gram: Can you speak French?
Greta: No. So I want to learn French.
Gram: Well...what do you want to do there?
Greta: I want to do my hair.
How about this style?
Gram: I think you need a lot of money. Do you have enough money?
Greta: That's a good question. In fact, that's a big problem.

[Track 38]

[GRAM Expressions]
get a haircut
go on a trip
go surfing
see some paintings
learn French
watch the fireworks

[Track 39]

Listen and number the pictures in order.

1. watch the fireworks
2. get a haircut
3. see some paintings
4. learn French
5. go surfing
6. go on a trip

[Track 40] p.65

[GRAM READING]

Listen to the story and answer the questions.

Early Vacation Planning…
Gramson, Greta and I are planning for our summer vacation.
We want to go to the mountain. We hope to go rafting. We also expect to sleep under the stars. Isn't this cool?
Greta decided to bring her tent. Gramson is planning to build a campfire.
Our summer vacation seems just perfect!
But, I almost forgot to check one thing; before the summer starts, we must get good grades on our exams.

[Track 41] p.68

Unit 11. Who Will Do The Presentation?

Listen to the dialogue.

Gram: Hey guys! Did you hear about the school cooking contest?
Gramson: No. When and where?
Greta: One month from now in the school hall.
Gram: I want to attend the contest. Can we work in groups?
Gramson: Cool! So what can we make?

Greta: How about a rainbow rice cake?
Gram: Great! Who will find the recipe?
Gramson&Greta: You can, Gram.
Gram: Good. Then who will do the presentation?
Gramson&Greta: Maybe...you can, Gram.
Gram: Then why work in a group?
Gramson: As your helpers,
Greta: we can try your food.

[Track 42]

[GRAM Expressions]
attend the contest
do the presentation
work in groups
win a contest
try food

[Track 43]

Listen and number the pictures in order.

1. try food
2. do the presentation
3. attend the contest
4. win a contest
5. work in groups

[Track 44] p.71

[GRAM READING]

Listen to the story and answer the questions.

- Cooking Contest Registration -

* Fill in the blanks and answer the questions to complete the form.
Team name: Gram Geeks.
Contestants: Gramson Brad, Gram Lee, and Greta Lee.
E-mail: gramgeek@grammar.net
Mobile phone: 080-3333-2222
Presentation: being ready
Entry Category: desserts
* What is your dish?
  Rainbow rice cake

* Where did you find your recipe?
  On the internet and from a Korean cook book.
* Why did you choose this dish?
  We wanted to show a healthy Korean traditional dessert.
* How can you make your dish?
  Please check the second file for the recipe.
* Which ingredients did you use? (3-4 ingredients)
  Rice flour, autumn squash, purple sweet potato, and raison.

[Track 45] p.74

Unit 12. If You Don't Hurry Up...

Listen to the dialogue.

Greta: Gram, if you don't mow the lawn, you won't get any pocket money.
Greta: Gram, if you watch TV too closely, you will have bad eye sight.
Greta: Gram, if you eat too much, you will feel very ill.
Gram: Where are my books?
Greta: Gram, if you don't tidy your room, you won't find your books.
Gram: Oh, I'm running out of time!
Greta: Gram, if you don't finish your homework like this, you will get bad grades.
Greta: If you don't hurry up,
Gramson: we will miss the movie!

[Track 46]

[GRAM Expressions]

Listen and repeat.

tidy her room
get bad grades
have bad eye sight
get pocket money
feel ill
mow the lawn

[Track 47]

Listen and number the pictures in order.

1. mow the lawn
2. get pocket money
3. have bad eye sight
4. feel ill
5. get bad grades
6. tidy her room

[Track 48] p.77

[GRAM READING]

Listen to the story and answer the questions.

- Instead Of My Family -

My bike is too old so I want a new one.
To buy my new bike, I'm planning to make some pocket money for it.
If I mow the lawn on Mondays, and if I wash the dishes on Tuesdays, and if I fix my cousin Gramson's model robot on Wednesdays, and if I do the laundry on Thursdays, and if I take out the trash on Fridays, and if I wash my dad's car on Saturdays, and if I water the plants on Sundays, then I will get 6,000 won per week!
Isn't this great? This is a perfect plan!

[Track 45] p.80

Unit 13. I Am As Tall As Steve

Listen to the dialogue.

Greta: Who is the boy in the picture?
Gram: He is my friend, Steve.
Greta: Oh, he is cool.
Gram: Look at me. I am as tall as Steve.
Greta: Are you as strong as Steve?
Gram: Yes, I am as strong as Steve.
Greta: Are you as smart as Steve?
Gram: Of course. I am as smart as Steve.
Gram: But... sometimes I am not as smart as Steve.

[Track 50]

[GRAM Expressions]

Listen and repeat.

strong
shy
smart
talkative
friendly
popular

[Track 51]

Listen and number the pictures in order.

1. strong
2. friendly
3. popular
4. shy
5. talkative
6. smart

[Track 52] p.83

[GRAM READING]

Listen to the story and answer the questions.

- Best Friends -

I'm Gram and my cousin is Gramson.
We look a lot different.
I'm 12 and he is 15.
I'm 5 feet tall. but I'm not as tall as him.
He's 6 feet tall.
Also I'm very talkative, so Gramson is not as talkative as me. He is quiet.
But we have one thing in common.
We both like cartoons.
I like cartoons as much as Gramson does.
That's why we can be best friends.

[Track 53] p.86

Unit 14. Which One Is Faster?

Listen to the dialogue.

Gram: Are you ready? Which one is shorter?
Greta: It's in your right hand.

Gram: Sorry, Greta. You're wrong. Give me one.
Greta: Here it is.
Gram: Then which one is faster?
Greta: It's in your...left hand.
Gram: Wrong! Give me two.
Greta: OK. Here you are.
Gram: Yoo-hoo! Are you ready again? Which one is higher?
Greta: Hmm... In your right hand! Yes, I'm right! Wow, I got a bonus. Give up all your cards, Gram!
Gram: Oh, my !

[Track 54]
[GRAM Expressions]
Listen and repeat.
fast or slow
expensive or cheap
fat or thin
young or old
hungry or full
high or low

[Track 55]
Listen and number the pictures in order.
1. high or low
2. young or old
3. expensive or cheap
4. fast or slow
5. hungry or full
6. fat or thin

[Track 56] Page 89
[GRAM READING]
Listen to the story and answer the questions.
- We Will Go To Gyeongju By Bus -
This weekend my family will go to Gyeongju.
My dad's car is more comfortable than a bus.
However, we will take an express bus.
Why? It is faster than driving.
There will be more cars on the road this weekend.
However, the bus uses the bus lane and it takes only four hours.
Taking a bus is also cheaper than driving.
I can't wait for the trip.

[Track 57] p.92

Unit 15. What Is The Tallest Tower?

Listen to the dialogue.
Greta: Hello and welcome to the Speed Quiz Show. Are you ready?
Greta: First. Which one of these is the oldest building?
Gramson: The pyramid is the oldest!
Greta: Right! You got one point, Gramson. Second. Which one of these is the tallest tower?
Gramson: The CN tower is the tallest!
Greta: Great, Gramson. Hello, Gram. Can you hear me?
Gram: Yes, I'm just warming up!
Greta: This is the last one. Who is the most famous singer...?
Gram: Gram! Gram!
Gramson: I am the most famous singer!

[Track 58]
[GRAM Expressions]
Listen and repeat.
hot or cold
old or new
wide or narrow
tall or short
heavy or light
famous

[Track 59]
Listen and number the pictures in order.
1. old or new
2. famous
3. heavy or light
4. tall or short
5. wide or narrow
6. hot or cold

[Track 60] p.95
[GRAM READING]
Listen to the story and answer the questions.
- Vincent van Gogh -
I went to the National Art Museum last Saturday.
There was a special exhibition.
It was the biggest Vincent van Gogh exhibition.
He didn't live a happy life, but he painted some of the most famous paintings in the world.
He is one of the greatest painters in history.
He is my favorite artist, too.
I was very happy to see Sunflowers, his most popular painting.

[Track 61] p.98

Unit 16. Have You Ever Cooked A Turkey?

Listen to the dialogue.
Greta: Gram, Gramson! Help me, please. It's about Thanksgiving dinner.
Gramson: OK.
Gram: What can I do for you?
Greta: Gram, have you ever baked a pumpkin pie?
Gram: Uh....no.
Greta: OK. Gramson, have you ever popped Indian popcorn?
Gramson: Indian popcorn? Well...no.
Greta: Fine. Gram, have you ever cooked a turkey?
Gram: That huge turkey you mean? No.
Greta: Come on! Then what have you ever done for Thanksgiving Day?
Gramson: We've eaten a lot turkey.
Gram: Every Thanksgiving Day.

[Track 62]

[GRAM Expressions]

Listen and repeat.

pop Indian popcorn

bake a pumpkin pie

cook a turkey

peel potatoes

keep a diary

eat with chopsticks

[Track 63]

Listen and number the pictures in order.

1. cook a turkey

2. pop Indian popcorn

3. eat with chopsticks

4. bake a pumpkin pie

5. peel potatoes

6. keep a diary

[Track 64] p.101

[GRAM READING]

Listen to the story and answer the questions.

- What We've Never Done -

Have you ever thought about what you've never done?

Gram's never baked a pie.

He's never kept a diary.

Gramson has never cleaned his room.

He's never eaten with chopsticks.

And what about me?

I've never been late for school.

I've never forgotten my brother's birthday.

I've never talked behind my brother's back.

Yes, I always talk to him openly.

Answers

Unit 01. I Want Some Cheese

[GRAM WORDS] p.8

6-3-1-4-2-5

[GRAM CHECK UP] p.9

1. We have **some** carrots.
2. I have **some** cheese.
3. Does Sarah have **any** oranges?
4. Do we have **any** milk?

[GRAM PRACTICE] p.10

A.

1. b**everages**   2. s**eafood**
3. m**eat**   4. d**airy** products
5. f**ruits**   6. v**egetables**

B.

1. some   2. some   3. any
4. some   5. any   6. some, any
7. some   8. any

[GRAM Comprehension] p.11

1. Yes. She needs some carrots.
2. No. She doesn't need any onions.
3. Yes. She needs some broccoli.

[GRAM Speaking] p.12

(A) some   (B) some
(C) any   (D) any

[GRAM Writing]

some fruits
some food
some vegetables
any bread

Unit 02. He Drinks A Lot Of Water

[GRAM EXPRESSIONS] p.14

3-6-1-5-2-4

[GRAM CHECK UP] p.15

1. Annie has **many** sweets.
2. We had **a lot of** steak.
3. How **much** milk do you drink a day?
4. How **many** oranges do you eat every day?

[GRAM PRACTICE] p.16

A.

1. junk food   2. steak & salad
3. nuts   4. rice & soup
5. sweets   6. coffee & tea

B.

1. many   2. many
3. many   4. many
5. much   6. much
7. many   8. much

[GRAM Comprehension] p.17

1. Yes. We should eat a lot of fresh fruits.
2. No. We should not eat much junk food.
3. Yes. Junk food has too many calories.

[GRAM Speaking] p.18

1. He has a lot of cookies.
2. She doesn't drink much water.
3. He has five oranges.

[GRAM Writing]

1. There was **a lot of** pizza.
2. His mom asked, "**How much** pizza did you eat?"
3. He answered, "I didn't eat **much pizza** because I wasn't hungry. I drank **a lot of coke**."

Unit 03. He Speaks English Well

[GRAM EXPRESSIONS] p.20

3-4-1-5-6-2

[GRAM CHECK UP] p.21

1. Gram always talks **loudly**.
2. Greta solves math problems **fast**.
3. Greta walks **slowly** in the classroom.
4. Greta sings **well**.

[GRAM PRACTICE] p.22

A.

1. Please **sit** down.
2. Please **raise** your hand.
3. Please **take** notes.
4. Please **solve** this problem.
5. Please **explain** to us.
6. Please **speak** in English.

B.

1. good ➜ well
   Kelly plays the piano well.
2. careful ➜ carefully
   We should take notes **carefully**.
3. hardly ➜ hard
   Nick always tries to study **hard**.
4. easy ➜ easily
   Mr. Hans explains English grammar **easily**.
5. quick ➜ quickly
   Please sit down **quickly** and read the questions.

[GRAM Comprehension] p.23

1. slowly ➜ quickly
   The students should take their seats **quickly**.
2. talk loudly ➜ raise their hands quietly
   The students should **raise their hands quietly** when they have a

question.

3. fast → quietly

The students should leave the classroom **quietly** after the test.

[GRAM Speaking] p.24

1. Yes, **she does. She studies hard.**

2. No, **she doesn't. She talks loudly.**

[GRAM Writing]

1. The boy is **listening** to the teacher **carefully**.

2. The girl is **doing** her homework **quickly**.

3. The two boys are **singing loudly**.

4. The girls are **talking quietly** to each other.

Unit 04. I Always Walk To School

[GRAM WORDS] p.26

5-2-4-1-6-3

[GRAM CHECK UP] p.27

1. I **always** watch TV at night.

2. Ben is **never** late for school

3. They **often** play soccer.

4. We **usually** go swimming.

[GRAM PRACTICE] p.28

A.

1. **pack** a schoolbag

2. do **homework**

3. go to **bed**

4. **take** a shower

5. **get** up

6. have **breakfast**

B.

1. I **often** have cereal for breakfast.

2. Warren **always** takes a shower after

dinner.

3. Alice and Jane are *never* late for school.

4. Paul **sometimes** goes to school by bus.

5. I **usually** pack my schoolbag before bed.

[GRAM Comprehension] p.29

1. Yes, he does.

2. No, he isn't. He is never late for school.

3. No, he doesn't. He always goes to bed before 10 o'clock.

[GRAM Speaking] p.30

(A) I **always wake up** at 7 in the morning.

(B) I wash my face. Then, I **sometimes eat cereal** for breakfast.

(C) I **often take the bus** to school, but today I walk to school. In the evening, I usually eat dinner at 6 p.m.

(D) Then I do my homework. My dad **always helps me** with my homework.

[GRAM Writing]

1. Gram **seldom has[eats] breakfast in the morning**.

2. Greta **is sometimes late for school**.

3. Gramson **always does his homework at night**.

Unit 05. I Am Milking A Cow!

[GRAM EXPRESSIONS] p.32

6-3-1-5-2-4

[GRAM CHECK UP] p.33

1. Gram **made some cookies**.

2. Greta **was dropping the eggs**.

3. Gramson **was washing the dishes in the kitchen**.

[GRAM PRACTICE] p.34

A.

1. **pick** apples

2. **gather** eggs

3. feed a **calf**

4. **unload** a truck

5. **milk** a cow

6. shear **sheep**

B.

1. Greta **picked some apples**.

2. Gramson **likes horses**.

3. Gram **is milking a cow**.

4. Greta **was reading a comic book**.

[GRAM Comprehension] p.35

1. They were milking a cow.

2. Gramson (He) kicked the egg basket.

3. Grandfather (He) hugged Gram and Gramson (them) smiling.

[GRAM Speaking] p.36

1. Gram **bought a hairband for Greta**.

2. Greta **asked a math problem to Gramson**.

3. Gramson **watched a horror movie**.

4. Greta **read a comic book yesterday**.

[GRAM Writing]

1. Gramson is **teaching English to Greta**.

2. Greta **bought a camera for Gram**.

3. Gramson **asked how to milk a cow**.

4. Gram **received a goose from Gramson**.

5. Gramson **made some cupcakes**.

Unit 06. My Friends Sent Me Presents

[GRAM EXPRESSIONS] p.38

3-5-6-2-4-1

[GRAM CHECK UP] p.39

1. Gramson **sells the girl his photos**.
2. Greta **gave the girl some cookies**.
3. Gram **teaches Gramson how to use the camera**.

[GRAM PRACTICE] p.40

A.

1. **show** Greta a model robot
2. lend Gram his **sneakers**
3. sell the girl his **photos**
4. give **Greta** a CD
5. pass Gram the **comic books**
6. **bring** the boy a T-shirt

B.

1. Greta **gave Gram some cookies**.
2. Gramson **found the boy his toy car**.
3. Gram **asked Greta a math problem**.

[GRAM Comprehension] p.41

1. Greta(She) brought her teacher a pink T-shirt.
2. A teacher taught them how to sell their things.
3. Gramson(He) sold a boy his model robot.

[GRAM Speaking] p.42

1. No, he didn't. He lent Gram his sneakers.
2. Gram(He) taught Greta French.
3. Gramson(He) bought Greta ice cream.

[GRAM Writing]

1. Gramson **bought Gram a robot magazine**. (D)
2. Greta **lent Gram a glove**. (E)

3. Gram **sent his friend an email**. (A)
4. Greta **showed Gram her new sneakers**. (C)
5. Gramson **gave Gram a hotdog**. (B)

Unit 07. Look At That Guy Playing The Guitar

[GRAM EXPRESSIONS] p.44

2-4-5-6-3-1

[GRAM CHECK UP] p.45

1. I saw Gram [to hold / **holding**] a sign in the concert.
2. Greta watched Gramson [**buy** / bought] some hotdogs.
3. Gramson listened to the girls [**shouting** / to shout].

[GRAM PRACTICE] p.46

A.

1. unfold a blanket
2. perform
3. go to a rock festival
4. wait in line
5. play Frisbee
6. hold a sign

B.

1. Greta **looked at Gram going to the rest room**.
2. Greta **saw Gram folding the blanket**.
3. Gramson **listened to Greta sing**.
4. Gram **felt Gramson looking at him**.

[GRAM Comprehension] p.47

1. No, (they didn't). They watched a (popular) band perform.
2. Gramson (He) looked at a girl holding a sign (in front of the stage).
3. They could see many people wait in line before the festival.

[GRAM Speaking] p.48

1. Gram watched Greta **taking** his guitar.
2. And he listened to Greta **playing** the guitar.
3. Suddenly Gram heard Greta **break** a string.
4. Then Gram saw Greta **running away**.

[GRAM Writing]

1. Gram's mom **felt Gram go out secretly**.
2. Greta **saw Gram eat pizza**.
3. Gramson **heard his cat crying under the bed**.
4. Gram **watched his team win the game**.

Unit 08. Please Make Greta Set The Table

[GRAM WORDS] p.50

3-2-4-1-5

[GRAM CHECK UP] p.51

1. Gram's mom let Gram [went / **go**] to the cinema.
2. Greta had a tooth [**filled** / filling].
3. Gramson made Greta [turned / **turn**] down the TV.

[GRAM PRACTICE] p.52

A.

1. **blow out** the candles
   → 촛불을 입으로 불어서 끄다.
2. **have** one's hair **cut** → 이발하다, 머리를 자르다
3. **decorate** the room → 방을 꾸미다
4. **clean up** the trash → 쓰레기를 치우다
5. **set** the table → 식탁을 차리다
6. **serve** the food → 음식을 대접하다

B.

1. Gram's dad **had Gram wash his car**.
2. The teacher **made Greta stay after class**.

3. Greta **let her brother use her phone**.

[GRAM Comprehension] p.53

1. **Gram had Greta set the table and food**.
2. Because **it rained heavily**.
3. Because **they ate too many sweets. (They had a lot of sweets)**.

[GRAM Speaking] p. 54

1. Gram **had Greta fix his guitar**.
2. Greta **let Gramson use her phone**.
3. Gramson **made Gram wait after school**.

[GRAM Writing]

1. Gram's mom **made Gram wash the dishes**.
2. Greta **let Gram use her bike**.
3. Gramson **had Gram feed his cat**.
4. Greta **made Gram clean up the trash**.

Unit 09. I Enjoy Watching Cartoons

[GRAM EXPRESSIONS] p.56

2-4-5-3-1-6

[GRAM CHECK UP] p.57

1. Greta doesn't like **getting up** early in the morning.
2. Gramson enjoys **baking** cookies.
3. Gram loves **drawing** a picture for his sister.

[GRAM PRACTICE] p.58

A.

1. watch cartoons
2. take a picture
3. make cupcakes
4. chat with
5. make a model airplane
6. play the guitar

B.

1. Gram enjoys **watching cartoons**.
   He likes **going** to the **cinema**.
2. Gramson enjoys **visiting Joe's Sweets store**.
   He loves **eating** chocolate.
3. Gram loves **learning** French.
   But he hates **studying math**.

[GRAM Comprehension] p.59

1. **Greta (She) hates trying on her dresses**.
2. **Gramson loves writing poems**.
3. **Gram enjoys writing stories for others**.

[GRAM Speaking] p.60

1. **I hate going out in the rain**.
2. **I enjoy listening to rock music**.
3. He **stops making so much noise**.
4. He **loves chatting with Gramson**.

[GRAM Writing]

2. He loves playing the guitar.
3. He hates studying math.
4. He likes going in-line skating.
5. He loves chatting with Gramson.
6. He likes writing stories.
7. He hates taking a shower.
8. He enjoys eating chicken.

Unit 10. I Want To Do My Hair

[GRAM WORDS] p.62

2-6-5-3-4-1

[GRAM CHECK UP] p.63

1. Gram wants **to eat** some hamburgers.
2. Gramson needs **to study** math more.

[GRAM PRACTICE] p.64

A.

1. watch the **fireworks**
2. go **surfing**
3. get a **haircut**
4. **learn** French
5. **go on** a trip
6. see some **paintings**

B.

1. Gram forgets **to feed** his dog.
2. Greta decided **to change** her hair style.
3. Gramson is learning **to play** the drums.
4. Greta wants **to go** to the Disneyland.

[GRAM Comprehension] p.65

1. They want to go to the mountain.
2. Greta decided to bring her tent.
3. Gramson plans to build a campfire.

[GRAM Speaking] p.66

1. Gram(He) wants to be a painter.
2. Greta(She) is planning to go scuba diving.
3. Gramson(He) wants to roast hot dogs.

[GRAM Writing]

2. She wants to swim with a dolphin.
3. She hopes to go to Paris this summer.
4. She promises to study hard.
5. She wants to ride on a motorboat.
6. She forgets to send Gram a birthday card.
7. She hopes to see the "Mona Lisa".
8. She promises to clean her room tonight.

Unit 11. Who Will Do The Presentation?

[GRAM EXPRESSIONS] p.68

3-2-5-4-1

[GRAM CHECK UP] p.69

1. **Who** won the contest?
2. **What** is your name?
3. **When** is your concert?
4. **Where** are you going?
5. **How** could you go there?
6. **Why** didn't you say so?

[GRAM PRACTICE] p.70

A.

1. do the **presentation**
   → 발표를 하다
2. **win** a contest
   → 대회에서 우승하다.
3. **attend** the contest
   → 대회에 참가하다.
4. work **in groups**
   → 그룹으로 활동하다
5. **try** food
   → 음식을 시식하다, 맛보다.
6. rainbow **rice cake**
   → 무지개 떡

B.

1. [**Who** / Which] likes rice cakes?
   → Gramson **likes rice cakes**.
2. [Who / **Whose**] laptop is this?
   → This **is Gram's laptop**.
3. [What / **How**] did Greta get good scores?
   → Greta **studied hard**.

[GRAM Comprehension] p.71

1. **Rainbow Rice Cake**
2. They found their recipe **on the internet and from a Korean cook book**.
3. They wanted to **show a healthy Korean traditional dessert**.

[GRAM Speaking] p.72

1. **How** did Greta **collect** information for making the rice cake?
   → She collected data **on the internet**.
2. **Where** did the kids **prepare** for the contest?
   → They prepared at **Gramson's** house.
3. **Who** helped to prepare the contest?
   → **Gramson's mom** helped them prepare for it.
4. **How** much rice flour did Gram use?
   → Gram used two **cups** of rice flour.

[GRAM Writing] p.72

contest
attend
What
When
Where
how

Unit 12. If You Don't Hurry Up…

[GRAM EXPRESSIONS] p.74

6-5-3-2-4-1

[GRAM CHECK UP] p.75

1. (If Gram tells it to the teacher) I will be in trouble.
2. You will get very cold (if you go out in the rain.)
3. I will show you my CDs (if you come to my house.)
4. (If we win the contest,) I'll have a party.

[GRAM PRACTICE] p.76

A.

1. mow the lawn
2. have bad eye sight
3. get bad grades
4. feel ill
5. tidy her room
6. get pocket money

B.

1. If it rains tomorrow, we **won't go to the beach**.
2. If you help me make cookies, we **will eat cookies together**.
3. If you practice playing the piano a lot, you **will be a pianist**.

[GRAM Comprehension] p.77

1. Gram **wants to make some pocket money for his new bike**.
2. If Gram **takes out the trash, he will get 500 won**.
3. If Gram **works instead of his family, he will get 6,000 won per week**.

[GRAM Speaking] p.78

1. If **it is sunny** tomorrow, they **will go in-line skating**.
2. Greta **will buy Gram ice cream** if Gram **helps** her do homework.
3. If **it rains** tomorrow, Gramson will **watch a video** at home.

[GRAM Writing]

2. If you study hard, you will pass the exam.
3. If you lie in the sun, you will get sunburned.
4. If you touch something hot, you will burn yourself.
5. If you eat too much, you will get fat.
6. If you don't listen in class, you won't (= will not) learn anything.

Unit 13. I Am As Tall As Steve

[GRAM EXPRESSIONS] p.80

1-4-6-5-2-3

[GRAM CHECK UP] p.81

1. Greta is **as popular as** Gramson.
2. Gram is **not as old as** Gramson.
3. Greta runs **as fast as** Gram.
4. Gram is **not as strong as** Greta.

[GRAM PRACTICE] p.82

A.

1. s**mart**　　2. f**riendly**
3. s**trong**　　4. t**alkative**
5. s**hy**　　6. p**opular**

B.

1. Yes. She **is as strong as** Gram.
2. Yes. He **sings as well as** Greta.
3. No. He **isn't as tall as** Gramson.
4. Yes. She **jumps as high as** Gram.
5. Yes. He **is as friendly as** Steve.
6. No. He **doesn't get up as early as** Gramson.

[GRAM Comprehension] p.83

1. No. Gram is 12 and Gramson is 15. (No. Gramson is not as old as Gram.)
2. No. Gram is not as tall as Gramson.
3. Yes. Gram likes cartoons as much as Gramson does.

[GRAM Speaking] p.84

1. No. She (Greta) is not as tall as her mom.
2. Yes. She (Greta) is as popular as Gramson.
3. No. She (Greta) doesn't (= does not) run as fast as Gram.

[GRAM Writing]

1. Gram **studies as hard as Steve**.
2. Gram **plays the guitar as well as Gramson**.
3. Gram **is not as strong as his dad**.

Unit 14. Which One Is Faster?

[GRAM WORDS] p.86

4-3-6-2-5-1

[GRAM CHECK UP] p.87

1. I'm [nicier / **nicer**] than you. Everybody loves me.
2. I'm [**smarter** / smartter] than

you and I'm [intelligenter / **more intelligent**] than you.

[GRAM PRACTICE] p.88

A.

1. **expensive** - (b)
2. **young** - (c)
3. **hungry** - (e)
4. **high** - (f)
5. **thin** - (g)
6. **slow** - (a)
7. **cheap** - (h)
8. **full** - (d)

B.

1. We arrived **earlier** than Susie.
2. Amy drives **more carefully** than Steven.
3. The train is **better than** the bus in many ways.
4. Traveling by an airplane is **quicker** than a car.

[GRAM Comprehension] p.89

1. They will go to Gyeongju this weekend.
2. They will take an express bus because it is faster than driving.
3. No. Taking a bus is cheaper than driving.

[GRAM Speaking] p.90

1. No, **he isn't**. Jihun **is shorter than** Chris.
2. No, **he isn't**. Ben **is fatter than Kevin**.
3. No, **he isn't**. Kevin **is weaker than** Jihun.

[GRAM Writing]

1. It **was slower than** the subway.
2. It **was more expensive** than the subway.
3. Unfortunately, they **arrived late** for the train.

[Crossword Puzzle] p.91

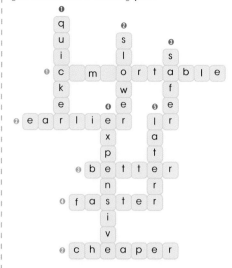

Unit 15. What Is The Tallest Tower?

[GRAM EXPRESSIONS] p.92

6-1-5-4-3-2

[GRAM CHECK UP] p.93

1. Who's the [**fattest** / fatest] amongst us? Is it you?
2. What? I have no idea but I think I'm the [most smart / **smartest**] and the [most prettiest / **prettiest**] of us.

[GRAM PRACTICE] p.94

A.

1. na**rrow** - (c)
2. **he**av**y** - (a)
3. fa**mous** - (f)
4. **wid**e - (h)
5. **light** - (b)
6. **c**old - (e)
7. **ta**ll - (d)
8. o**ld** - (g)

B.

1. Brad is **the oldest** boy.
2. Ken has **the longest** hair.
3. Andy is **the smartest** boy.
4. **Andy** has the shortest hair.
5. David is **the youngest** and **the**

fattest boy.

[GRAM Comprehension] p.95

1. He went to the National Art Museum (to see the Vincent van Gogh exhibition).
2. Yes. He is one of the greatest painters in history.
3. He saw Sunflowers, Vincent van Gogh's most popular painting.

[GRAM Speaking] p.96

(A) Gram said, "**The widest river** is the Amazon river, right?"
(B) Gramson said, "Right. But it's not **the longest** one."
(C) Greta said, "Really? Then **what** is the longest?"
  Gramson said, "The Nile is the longest."
(D) Gram said, "And it's one of **the oldest** rivers, too."

[GRAM Writing]

2. Gram bought **the most expensive** sneakers **in the store**.
3. Death Valley in California is **the hottest** place **in California**.
4. This road is **the narrowest** road **in my town**.
5. Yuna Kim is **the best** figure skater **in the world**.
6. The blue whale is **the heaviest** animal **of all the sea animals**.

[Hidden Word] p.97

① shiest
② proudest
③ happiest
④ coldest
⑤ driest
⑥ slowest
⑦ fattest
⑧ thinnest

⑨ wildest
⑩ heaviest
⑪ angriest
⑫ hottest

Unit 16 Have You Ever Cooked A Turkey?

[GRAM EXPRESSIONS] p.98

2-4-1-5-6-3

[GRAM PRACTICE] p.100

A.

1. cook a **turkey** / 칠면조를 요리하다
2. **bake** a pumpkin pie / 호박파이를 굽다
3. eat **with** chopsticks / 젓가락으로 음식을 먹다
4. **pop** Indian popcorn / 인디언 옥수수로 팝콘을 만들다
5. **keep** a diary / 일기를 쓰다
6. **peel** potatoes / 감자껍질을 깎다(벗겨내다).

B.

1. Gram has [helpped / **helped**] Greta.
2. Gramson has [**drunk** / drank] a carton of milk.
3. Greta has [being / **been**] to Paris.
4. Gram has [**eaten** / ate] sushi.

[GRAM Comprehension] p.101

1. No. He(Gram) has (He's) never kept a diary.
2. No. He(Gramson) has (He's) never cleaned his room.
3. No. She(Greta) has (She's) never forgotten her brother's birthday.

[GRAM Speaking] p.102

1. Greta **has been to London**. (C)
2. No, **he hasn't**. (B)
3. Yes, **he has**. (A)
4. Gram **has read Hamlet**. (D)

[GRAM Writing]

Have
Been
prepared
baked
has
peeled

Index

GramGram Plus 4

First Printing 2014.8.20

Author Hyunjeong, Kim

Illustration SeokHi, Kim

Consultant Prof. Eunyoung, Park

Editorial Supervisor LLS English Research Center

Publisher Kiseon, Lee

Publishing Company JPLUS

62, World Cup-ro 31-gil, Mapo-gu, Seoul, Korea

Telephone 02-332-8320

Fax 02-332-8321

Homepage www.jplus114.com

Registration Number 10-1680

Registration Date 1998.12.09

ISBN 979-11-5601-019-7

ⓒ JPLUS 2014

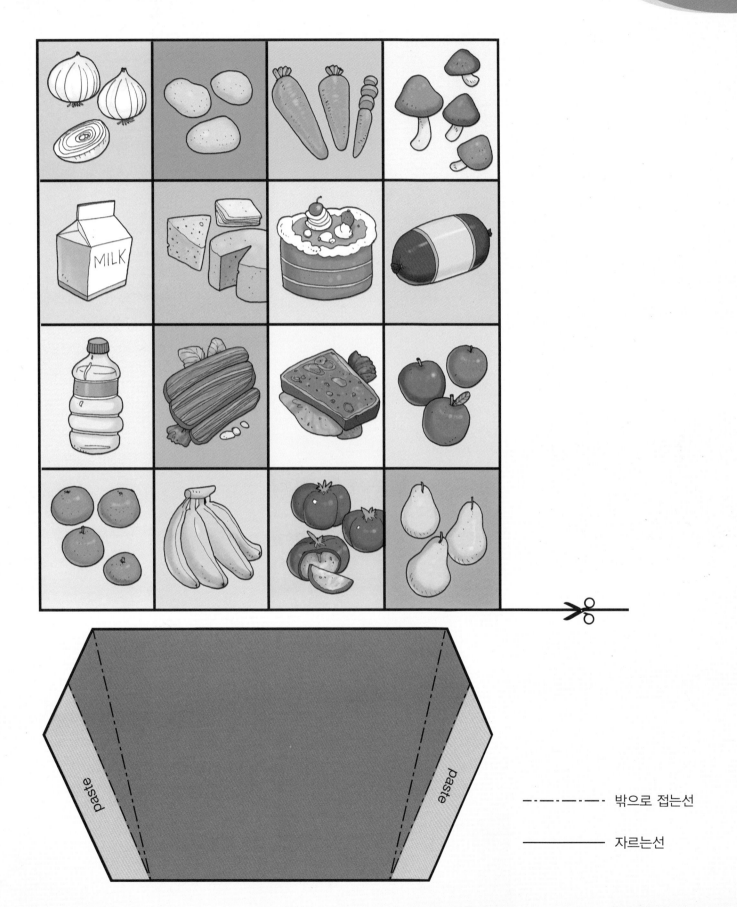

---·---·--- 밖으로 접는선

————— 자르는선

mushrooms	carrots	potatoes	onions
ham	cake	cheese	milk
apples	beef	pork	water
pears	tomatoes	bananas	oranges

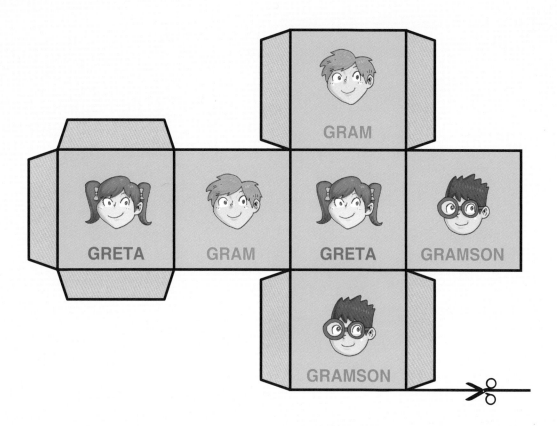

GRAM

GRETA   GRAM   GRETA   GRAMSON

GRAMSON

JOB DONE	JOB DONE	JOB DONE	JOB DONE	JOB DONE
JOB DONE	JOB DONE	JOB DONE	JOB DONE	JOB DONE
JOB DONE	JOB DONE	JOB DONE	JOB DONE	JOB DONE
JOB DONE	JOB DONE	JOB DONE	JOB DONE	JOB DONE

Unit 06 To The Right Person! p.43

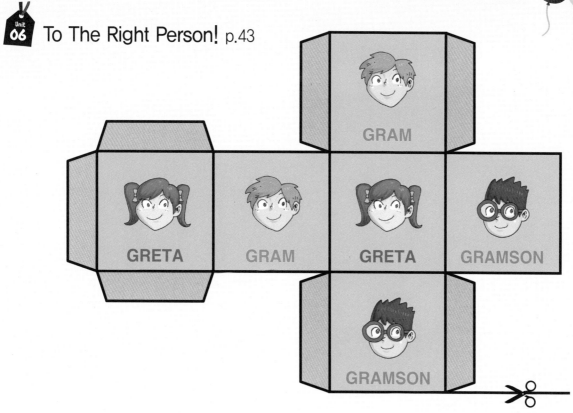

I Did It!	I Did It!	I Did It!
I Did It!	I Did It!	I Did It!
I Did It!	I Did It!	I Did It!
I Did It!	I Did It!	I Did It!

FUNNY GRAM

GramGram Plus 4

Unit 08 Light Up The Candles! p.55

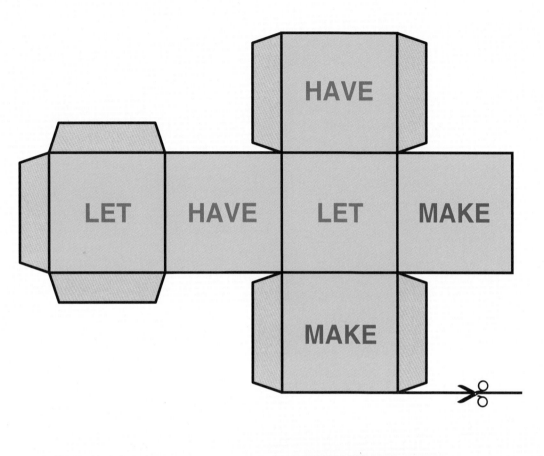

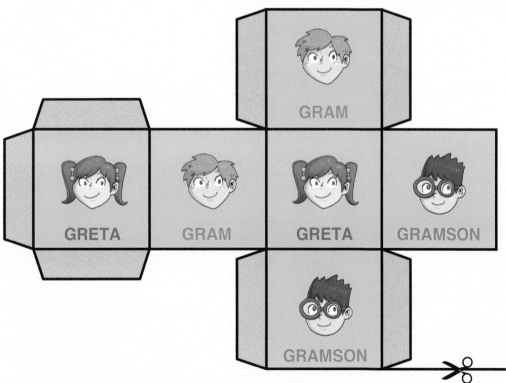

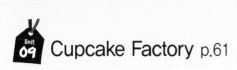

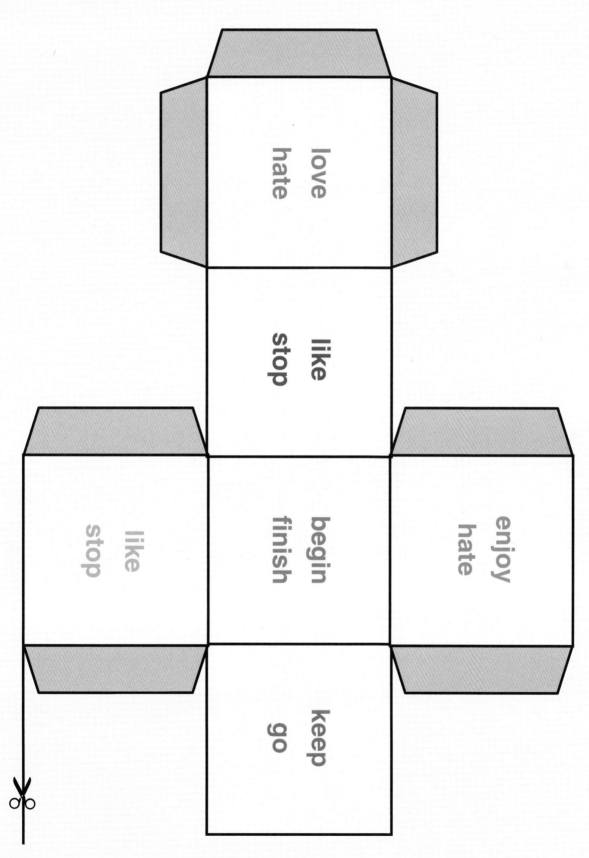

Unit 11 Sweet Mini Pie Time p.73

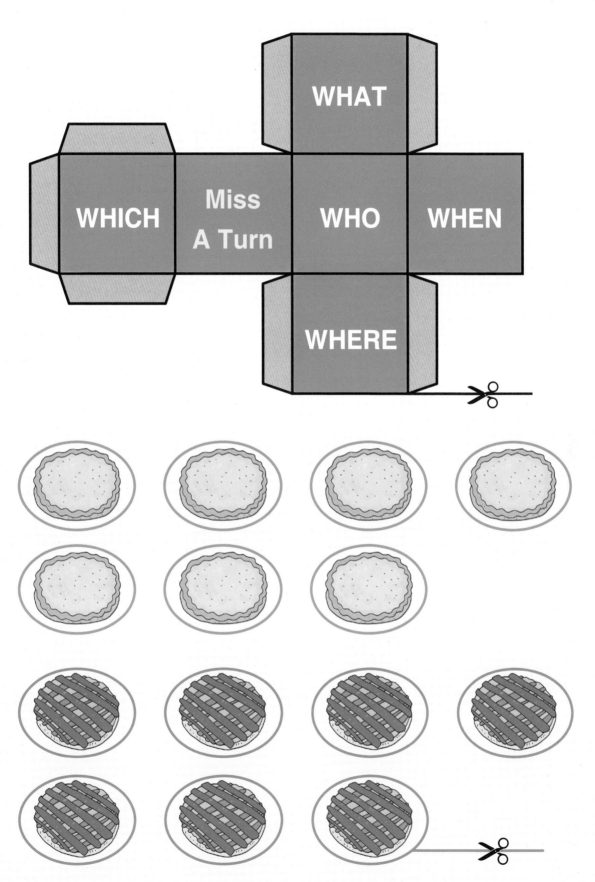

WHAT

WHICH | Miss A Turn | WHO | WHEN

WHERE

If you don't listen in class,	If you don't tidy your room,	If you lie in the sun,
If you don't take an umbrella,	If you eat too much,	If you don't take your medicine,
If you don't hurry up,	If you save up your money,	If you watch TV too closely,
If you mow the lawn,	If you miss the bus,	If you practice playing the piano a lot,
If it is sunny,	If you don't brush your teeth,	If it rains tomorrow,

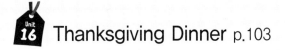

Unit 16 Thanksgiving Dinner p.103

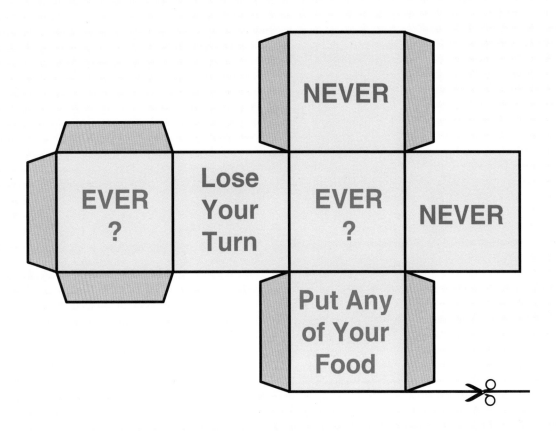

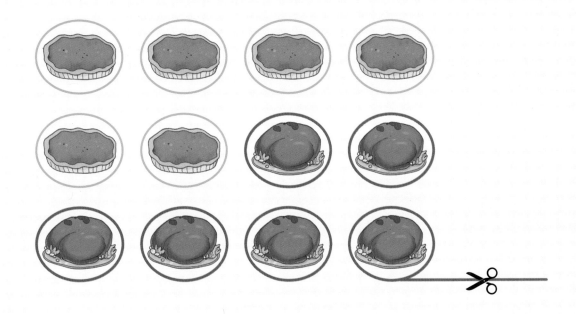